SpringerBriefs in Computer Science

For further volumes:
http://www.springer.com/series/10028

Markus Jakobsson

Mobile Authentication

Problems and Solutions

 Springer

Markus Jakobsson
PayPal
San Jose
CA, USA

ISSN 2191-5768   ISSN 2191-5776 (electronic)
ISBN 978-1-4614-4877-8   ISBN 978-1-4614-4878-5   (eBook)
DOI 10.1007/978-1-4614-4878-5
Springer New York Heidelberg Dordrecht London

Library of Congress Control Number: 2012942921

Printed on acid-free paper

Springer is part of Springer Science+Business Media (www.springer.com)

For A and Art.

Foreword

"Something you are; something you know; something you have." – I first heard these words as a graduate student studying computer security technologies and authentication. These three factors are all we have at our disposal to try to correctly identify other human beings.

In face-to-face interaction, familiar people use "something you are" to identify one another such as their facial structure or voices. When driving through an EZPass toll booth, one uses "something you have" to identify one's car, so that the appropriate account is billed. And when logging into most websites, users typically use "something you know" as the password. Using multiple factors in combination is known to increase security.

While most facets of technology have advanced exponentially, authentication of people to machines has stagnated for quite some time. Most people still use conventional passwords to log into websites for shopping, banking, and other sensitive transactions. We are starting to see small advances in practice, typically in the form of two-factor authentication instead of one, but we have not had the kind of revolution that other areas of technology have enjoyed.

In his new book featuring "duets" with several of his co-authors, Markus Jakobsson gives a fascinating look at current and potential future authentication technologies. He explains why the problem of authenticating users to machines is so difficult and gives a peek under the hood of some of the more promising techniques. For example, while many consider biometrics to be the holy grail for authentication, this book highlights the real benefits as well as the limitations of these techniques.

This book offers a deep understanding of password and PIN schemes and also covers such topics as visual authentication and defeating spoofing. Whether you are a practitioner who needs to understand your options for authenticating users, or a computer scientist who wants to perform research on this important and interesting topic, this book has plenty to offer you.

As a security professional, I began reading this book thinking that it would be a review of concepts I was already familiar with, but I found that I learned a tremendous amount, and think that this book is a must have for anyone in the security field.

Baltimore, May 2012 *Avi Rubin*

Preface

As a society, we have used different forms of authentication since ancient times – of people, documents, materials of value, etc. With the emergence of networked computers in the latter part of the twentieth century, authentication research flourished and many new techniques were developed. Among the central concepts developed or improved upon, we find PINs, passwords, various forms of backup authentication, techniques for device identification, and cryptographic techniques for message authentication.

While consumer habits and the use of legacy systems have hampered changes to authentication systems, we argue that systems designed with these issues in mind can be successfully deployed, and help address global security issues of increasing importance. In this book, we support this argument by describing a collection of new authentication technologies to address unmet authentication needs in a way that minimizes friction, and experimental evaluations of the technologies to quantify the benefits of deployment.

A handset is not just a small computer – it is a small computer with a different user interface. People use it differently. Therefore, mobile authentication is not simply authentication on a mobile device – there are other constraints and enablers. This book focuses on mobile authentication.

While this book provides a view of frontiers in authentication research, we certainly do not make any claims of covering all angles. However, we hope to convince the reader of the value of departing from the status quo and adopting new authentication methods.

Mountain View, California,
May, 2012

Markus Jakobsson
Principal Scientist of Consumer Security, PayPal

Acknowledgements

This book would not have been possible without the contributions of my co-authors – Ruj Akavipat, Mayank Dhiman, Debin Liu, Saman Gerami Moghaddam, Mohsen Sharifi and Hossein Siadati. We have benefitted from insightful discussions with Dirk Balfanz, Jeff Edelen, Aaron Emigh, Nathan Good, William Leddy, Brett McDowell, Jim Palmer, Garry Scoville, and Diana Smetters. Many thanks to Dahn Tamir, who helped in the execution of experiments involving Amazon Mechanical Turk, and to Hampus Jakobsson for assistance with recruiting subjects. We also appreciate the helpful feedback we have received from participants in the user studies underlying many of the chapters. Also, we wish to thank Jeff Hodges, M. Mannan, Netanel Raisch, and Chris Schille for feedback on earlier drafts; Hossein Siadati for LaTex assistance; and Eric Park for editorial guidance. Last but not least, thanks to Michael Barrett for recognizing the benefits of both basic and applied research at Paypal, thereby enabling much of this work.

Contents

Chapter 1
The Big Picture

Authentication is one of the issues at the heart of machine security, and there is a great array of authentication types. To begin with, one can classify authentication methods based on who is authenticating to whom, creating a breakdown into *machine-to-machine* authentication, *machine-to-human* authentication, *human-to-human* authentication, and *human-to-machine* authentication.

Practically speaking, machine-to-machine authentication is well understood. While there is a great number of types, properties, and designs of digital signatures and message authentication codes, there is little commercial demand for improvement. This might mean that we have achieved something close to perfection, or it might simply mean that we are currently satisfied with what we have. Similarly, there is rather limited activity related to machine-to-human authentication. This is a form of authentication that is relatively rare, and mostly used in the context of authenticating a service provider to an end user to avoid attackers from successfully impersonating service providers – as is done in a typical phishing attack. Human-to-human authentication is potentially of great interest in the context of recommendation systems, where the authentication is not of a particular individual as much as of an individual of a particular group; that, however, is outside the scope of this book. This book is about *human-to-machine* authentication, with a focus on the mobile scenario.

Human-to-machine authentication is a very active research area at the time of writing, with a tremendous number of publications related to passwords alone. But human-to-machine authentication is not synonymous to password research; one goal of this book is to make that point. Human-to-machine authentication is a startlingly complex issue. In the *old* days of computer security – before 2000 – the human component was all but disregarded. It was either assumed that people should *and would* be able follow instructions, or that end users were hopeless and would always mess up. The truth, of course, is somewhere in between, which is exactly what makes this so enticing. We cannot make progress with human-to-machine authentication without understanding *both humans and machines*. How can we design secure systems that take into consideration that end users are *people*? People like you and me, but also people *unlike* you and me.

M. Jakobsson, *Mobile Authentication*, SpringerBriefs in Computer Science,
DOI: 10.1007/978-1-4614-4878-5_1, © The Author(s) 2013

I am not making any claims whatsoever at covering the vast expanse of research done in the field of human-to-machine authentication. Instead, this book is written to highlight how many aspects there are to this problem. My aim is to convey the complexity of the issue, and the beauty of looking further into what things *mean* – as opposed to simply what they look like. You will find me peeking often into the mind of the end user throughout the book, arguing both about *what* people do and *why* they do it. I do not believe we can make progress without understanding the problem. The problem, here, is not only what we want to achieve – but equally important, how all the components work. And in particular, how the *human* component works. That said, this is not a psychology book. It is a computer security book that refuses to let go of the question, *"What do people do, and why?"*

The book consists of a collection of short chapters that I co-authored with some of my colleagues who are as passionate about these questions as I am. Each chapter is intended to bring light to one or more questions of relevance to human-to-computer authentication. Each chapter, you may say, argues a point that I feel is worth keeping in mind.

The book begins by describing a neglected aspect of passwords – *how they are made.* It seems embarrassingly obvious to state, but passwords are made by *people.* They are not random strings of characters. People use mental rules when they produce passwords – they concatenate, insert, and modify *components.* These components are typically words, sometimes numbers, and sometimes – typically due to demands from the service providers – other characters. But if that is so, why are we measuring strength in terms of the number of letters and digits? Should we not instead look at the commonality of the components, and the way in which these were combined? Chapter 2 shares some insights that can be gained by looking just at how passwords were made. While this chapter speaks of universal truths, it is well understood that people choose worse passwords in mobile contexts – it is so painful to enter complex passwords there. That makes it even more important to understand what passwords are strong enough, and which ones are not.

Chapter 3 takes a look at PINs. But perhaps not from the perspective you might expect. Instead, the question is asked: what can an organization do when its users have *passwords*, but *need* PINs? It presents a very simple approach by which an organization can bootstrap PIN ownership without any notable use friction. By doing so, it pays attention to maybe the most important issue of applied security: *If it is not easy to use, it will not be used.*

In chapter 4, several questions are asked and answered. Among these are *"How can we obtain more secure human-to-machine authentication?"*; *"How can we improve recall rates?"*; and *"How do we make it easy to authenticate using a handset?"*. As proposed in chapter 2, the search for answers start with the end user. What makes credentials secure? What makes them easy to remember? And what makes them easy to enter in devices with constrained user interfaces?

Chapter 5 pays special attention to the problem of memorability. It is believed that preferences are more stable than long-term memory. If you liked tennis two years ago, you probably still like tennis. And if you disliked olives last year, that is probably still true. People change, but surprisingly little! An authentication scheme based on preferences can also be more resistant to data-mining efforts than knowledge-based approaches to password reset, in spite of the tremendous amounts of personal information that many typical Internet users share over social networks. This chapter shows how one can create a usable and secure authentication scheme based on preferences. In other words, it is not only about what people can do, but also about *who they are*.

One aspect that is often neglected when people speak about authentication is how to avoid abuse. Phishing, at its heart, is an *abuse* of authentication mechanisms. Chapter 6 describes how an understanding of spoofing can help us change how people authenticate, turning a liability into an asset by making a system in which lack of attention and dependence on habits no longer pose a threat, but become a benefit. This chapter therefore emphasizes the importance of understanding *how and why people fail* – and take that into consideration when designing secure systems.

In chapter 7, we ask: What problems and inconveniences can be addressed by a complete architectural redesign of a system? In particular, given a device with a biometric reader – such as a fingerprint scanner – what can we achieve? And what are the potential problems that may *arise* from a large-scale deployment of biometric readers – and how can these be proactively addressed? Society is rapidly moving towards an increased use of biometrics. We can use such devices the right way – or in less desirable ways. If we understand the issues at stake – issues as diverse as those arising from phishing attacks and replacement of devices – then we can produce a solution that does not simply replace passwords, but which creates new benefits.

Finally, we consider what can be done in a world inhabited by legacy servers. A complete redesign of the Internet and everything that connects to it may solve many of our problems in a very elegant way – but is this an approach that we can meaningfully expect? Chapter 8 describes how one can change the world while respecting legacy servers. I am *certain* that the approach I will describe cannot be used to achieve *any* change we may hope to make – but this book is about inspiration and first steps!

Chapter 2
The Benefits of Understanding Passwords

Markus Jakobsson, Mayank Dhiman

Abstract

In an effort to assess the strength of passwords, password strength checkers count lower-case and upper-case letters, digits and other characters. However, this does not truly measure how likely a given password is. To determine the likelihood of a password, one must first understand how passwords are generated – this chapter takes a first step in that direction. This is particularly important in a mobile context, where users already are tempted to use short and simple passwords – given how arduous password entry is.

2.1 Why We Need to Understand Passwords

While we do not think that passwords are the best way for people to authenticate to their devices and service providers, it is important to recognize the degree to which passwords are part of infrastructure, which makes them difficult to replace – even if we agree on what to replace them with.

This chapter describes a new method by which we can address two common problems relating to traditional passwords. The first problem is that of approximating the security of a given credential. Traditional password strength checkers plainly demand the presence of certain predicates – such as a combination of uppercase and lowercase; the inclusion of numerals; and that passwords do not match any of the most common passwords (such as "abc123"). This is not necessarily the optimal strategy, as it does not capture common transformations (such as from to common password "password" to the very similar "passw0rd"). Rather than extending the blacklist to all common variants of all common passwords, it is better to understand the underlying structure of passwords, and how people generate them. This allows us to score passwords based on how they were generated – doing this allows us to determine that "p1a2s3s4w5o6r7d" is somehow less secure than "a1d9o8g4." Without an understanding of how passwords are generated, the former password is likely to be believed to be the stronger of the two. (Of course, if mindless exhaustive search is the only path of compromise, the former password *is* the strongest of the two – so security must be seen in context of the most prevalent threat.)

M. Jakobsson, *Mobile Authentication*, SpringerBriefs in Computer Science,
DOI: 10.1007/978-1-4614-4878-5_2, © The Author(s) 2013

The second problem this chapter addresses is how to identify credential reuse – whether sequentially for one account, or consecutively between two or more accounts. Here, we do not only consider *verbatim* reuse, but also *approximate* reuse – such as "BigTomato" and "bigTOMATO1." If a person has two accounts with different passwords then loses one of the passwords to a fraudster, then the fraudster has a reasonable chance to get access to the other account as well. This is because the attacker may try all common transformations of the stolen credential, hoping that one of them will work for the second account. As a result, we need to identify and discourage both verbatim and approximate password reuse. While verbatim reuse can be detected without any understanding of the underlying credentials, detection of approximate reuse requires a structural understanding of passwords.

The two techniques described herein are closely related, and are both based on the parsing and decomposition of passwords, using rules matching those people are relying on when they *generate* passwords. Examples of such rules are insertion of one component into another component; concatenation of components; and common transformations of elements of a component.

2.2 People Make Passwords

A good password is hard to guess. Conversely, of course, a bad password is *easy* to guess. But what is it that makes something hard to guess, and how can we tell?

It is easier to tell that something is *easy* to guess than that it is hard to guess. For example, the following potential passwords are easy to guess: *fraternity* (a dictionary word); *$L* (a very short string); *qwertyuiop* (a string with a very predictable pattern); and *LoveLoveMeDo* (famous lyrics). Similarly, one can look at the commonality of passwords – any user who wants to use a password that has already reached the limit has to think of another password. This approach is taken by Schechter, Herley, and Mitzenmacher [81]. We can make a long list of reasons to consider a password to be weak – and this is what typical password strength checkers do – but how can we tell that we have not missed some?

To be able to determine what makes most sense, we need to understand how passwords are constructed. Passwords are constructed by *people*, and people follow guidelines and mental protocols when performing tasks. Therefore, a better understanding of passwords requires a better understanding of people – or at least how people construct passwords.

To gain a better understanding of this, we collected a very large number of actual passwords. We sampled and reviewed these, thinking carefully about how each password was constructed. It is meaningful to think of passwords as strings that are composed of *components*, where components are *dictionary words*, *numbers*, and *other characters*. When producing a password, a typical user composes a password from a small number of such components using one or more *rules*.

The most common rule is *concatenation*, followed by *replacement*, *spelling mistake*, and *insertion*. Here, an example of a concatenation is producing "passbay1" from the three components "pass," "bay," and "1." Use of *L33T*[1] is a common replacement strategy, creating "s3v3nty" from "seventy" by replacement of each "e" with a "3." Misspellings may be intentional or unintentional, resulting in passwords such as "clostrofobic." Finally, insertion produces strings such as "Christi77na," where "77" was inserted into the name "Christina." (This was the least common type of rule among those we surveyed and the hardest to automatically detect in practice, so this rule was not used in the experiment we describe herein.)

The simple insight that *people* choose passwords suggests a new approach to determining the strength of a password: One can determine the components making up the password and the commonality of each such component; one could then consider the mental generation rules used to combine the components and make up the password – along with the commonality of these rules being used. The strength of the password, in some sense, depends directly on the commonality of the password, which in turn depends on the commonality of its components and password generation rules. Similarly, when determining the similarity of two passwords, one can compare the components that make up the two passwords along with the generation rules. It is therefore important to understand the commonality of components and rules.

2.3 Building a Parser

Components and Rules

To build a parser, we need to understand the components and the generation rules, and then "decompile" passwords into the components they were made from. We will therefore review how most passwords are formed, in order to understand how to invert this process.

Examples

- **Concatenating components.** The password "mylove123" consists of three components: "my," "love," and "123" combined with two occurrences of the concatenation rule. By determining the observed frequencies of the three components and the concatenation rule, it is possible to assess the "likelihood" of the password.
- **Order matters.** The password "my123love" has the same components and uses the same rules – except it does not attach the numerals at the end. A simple analysis of passwords shows that most passwords containing numerals have them at the end. And since the goal of parsing is to assess the likelihood of a given password – its believed strength – we see that order matters. Put a different way,

---

[1] L33T is pronounced "leet," and is a relatively common transcription of words in which letters are replaced by other characters with some resemblance to the replaced letter.

the "value" of the component "123" is greater when it is not at the end of the password.

- **Insertion.** Next, the password "mylo123ve" is even stronger, given that it does not only use concatenation but also insertion: the user has inserted the component "123" inside the component "love," which, in turn, was concatenated to the component "my."

- **L33T and multiple parsing possibilities.** The password "myl0v3" has two components, "my" and "l0v3," where the second component is L33T for "love." Here however, "l0v3" can either be seen as a dictionary word whose frequency is recorded and used to score passwords in which it occurs, or it can be seen as the result of a L33T-rule applied to a dictionary word. While the former approach is more straightforward, it does not benefit from knowledge of the observed frequencies of the underlying words. The latter approach, on the other hand, may result in errors where the L33T term is more common – relatively speaking – than the associated word. One approach to address this is to parse the password both ways and use the more conservative assessment.

- **Maximizing coverage.** Finally, the password "thinput" shows that there could be multiple paths. This could either be the result of concatenating the two character components "t" and "h" with the component "input," or it could be the result of concatenating "thin" and "put." Like in the previous example, it is possible to produce multiple parsing results and then select the most conservative. In the parser we describe, though, a greedy word-based approach was taken, where passwords are considered combinations of the words that "cover" the biggest portion of the strings. This is a result of the observation that most passwords are based on words, which surely is due to the fact that people relate better to words with meaning than to strings of random characters.

What the Parser Does

The parser takes a password as input and outputs the various components and rules which have been used to construct that password – or *appear* to have been used, to be specific. As we have mentioned, components include words, numbers, individual characters, and special symbols. Some components may be overlapping, e.g., a word is made up of number of characters. In such cases, those components are parsed first which have longer length. This minimizes the number of components that are used to "cover" the credential.

The parser has built-in rules to identify three major password creation rules: *concatenation*, *L33T*, and *misspelling*.

In order to parse an input, the parser uses an *input dictionary*. It is worth noting that language has strong influence on the creation of passwords and that words usually form the core around which various other operations are applied to make the password more complex. For simplicity, only English dictionaries are used herein.

The *input dictionary* contains words from different sources, such as a standard English dictionary, people's first and last names, geographical locations, technical terminology, and so forth. A vanilla English dictionary is not sufficient because many passwords contain words and phrases from the latter categories. To achieve a better and more comprehensive dictionary, we combined specialized dictionaries based on such topics. The final dictionary obtained upon merging these specialized dictionaries contained just below 670,000 words.

The parser contains algorithms capable of identifying password creation rules. The parser uses the input dictionary and the specified algorithms to identify the components and rules for the input password. The detection of components is directly dependent upon the choice of input dictionary.

Note that in many cases the passwords can be broken into components in more than one way. In such cases, the parser selects the components containing words with the *maximum coverage*. Maximum coverage means that the total length of the combined components, which are words, is maximized. For example, "thinput" will get parsed as "thin" and "put" rather than "t," "h," and "input." When two paths produce the same coverage, the path with the greatest probability of occurrence (as judged by the frequency of use of the rules and components) is chosen. Practically speaking, this typically corresponds to the path with the smallest number of components. Therefore, "password123" will be parsed as "password" and "123," rather than "pass," "word," and "123." The details of how the parser operates are given the next subsection.

Parsing Details

The three main subroutines which are required for parsing components are *generate-all-substrings*, *generate-max-substrings* and *generate-leftover-components*, which we will describe in detail next.

Consider a potential password "hello1." A call to *generate-all-substrings* will generate all possible substrings of a given string. Hence, a call to *generate-all-substrings* using this input generates "h," "e," "l," "o," "1," "he," "el," "ll," ..., "hello," "ello1," "hello1."

The *generate-max-substrings* subroutine takes in a password as an input and generates a set of substrings, which are words and can be found in the input dictionary. Only that set of substrings is returned which provides the *maximum coverage* of the input string. For example, using *generate-all-substrings* as a subroutine, and an input "hello2(world!35b," the subroutine *generate-max-substrings* returns a list containing "hello" and "world."

The third subroutine *generate-leftover-components* requires two arguments: the password and the list of substrings generated by *generate-max-substrings* using the password as an input. This subroutine will return the remaining components – i.e., consecutive numbers, characters and special symbols – after cutting the substrings generated by *generate-max-substrings* from the password. Thus, calling *generate-*

leftover-components with the inputs of "hello2(world!35b" and ["hello," "world"] returns "2," "(,""!," "35," and "b." Notice that the string is broken up into conceptually consistent pieces – e.g., "!35b" is split into "!," "35," and "b."

Regular Components and Concatenation

In order to identify the components, the parser first checks if the password can be found in the input dictionary. In that case, the password contains only one component, the password itself. For example, "monkey" is one of the most commonly used passwords, which can be found in the dictionary. In the next step, the parser checks if the password contains numbers only. For example, keyboard patterns like "12345" and dates of birth are quite common passwords. The first two steps are performed in this order due to efficiency reasons. This is because an average of 25% of all passwords in most datasets are either dictionary words or complete numbers.

In order to detect concatenation, the parser uses the *generate-max-substrings* subroutine described above, which generates the set of substrings that provide *maximum coverage*. These results are combined with the results of *generate-leftover-components* to generate all the components of the password.

Identifying L33T

Since, L33T is not a proper language and many different dialects of L33T occur on the Internet, there is no perfect algorithm to convert between English and L33T. Since the rules for such conversion vary, one can use an exhaustive approach. One can construct a table containing all mappings from a token to be replaced (number or special symbol) to a list of all common replacements for that token, as seen in various L33T to English translators. For example, the character "0" is substituted for "o" and the character "|" can be substituted for both "i" and "l." Hence, in the mapping table there will be an entry for "@" to be mapped to "a" and "|" to be mapped to both "i" and "l."

Identification of L33T works in combination with the *generate-max-substrings* subroutine. The *generate-max-substrings* subroutine tries to replace the tokens with all possible characters found in the mapping of token in the L33T to English mapping table. All possible combinations are tried. For each combination tried, the parser tries to find the maximum covering strings. If the new substrings generated covers a larger length than the previously calculated substrings, then that character is replaced by the new character from the mapping. Consider the password "||ovey0u." Each token which is not a letter is considered for replacement – in this example, there are three such characters. For each combination of "reasonable" substitutions, *generate-max-substrings* is run. The substitution with the greatest coverage is selected and output; in our example, "||ovey0u" would be converted to "iloveyou," which then would broken into the three words it consists of.

Identifying Spelling Mistakes

Identification of spelling mistakes is more complex. Initially, the *generate-max-substrings* subroutine is called and the output of it is then used as input for the *generate-leftover-components* subroutine in order to examine leftover components. For example, consider the password "heilloworld." A call to *generate-max-substrings* will generate "world" which along with the initial password is used as an input to *generate-leftover-components* which will generate "heillo." This is the leftover string and potentially contains a spelling mistake. Before starting to parse the passwords, a training module is used to train for detection of spelling mistakes using an input dictionary. There is another component of this training module, which tries to detect and correct the spelling of each component, if possible. In case a spelling mistake is found, then a new string is generated in which the spelling mistake has been rectified, and the subroutine *generate-max-substrings* is called for a second time using this new string. This is because in certain cases, the incorrectly spelled word may be used to create longer words. For example, "jidgement" will initially generate the component "gem," but after the spelling mistake has been rectified, calling *generate-max-substrings* will generate "judgement."

2.4 Building a Model

The parser we have described can be used to process large sets of passwords, producing the associated components and rules used to produce the passwords in the sets. By recording the frequencies of each of the components observed – and the rules that were used – one can produce a stochastic model for how passwords are generated. This model can then be used to score passwords. In the following, we will describe how to build the model.

Approach

In order to build a model of passwords, one needs a large collection of passwords and an input dictionary. One can use any set of passwords to train the system. The larger the dataset is, the more accurate the resulting frequency database will be. If one small dataset is considered higher quality – i.e., more accurate – than a larger dataset, then one can perform "weighted" training using both. In the example we describe, however, we only used one dataset for training: The *RockYou dataset*. The RockYou dataset contains 32 million passwords, leaked in 2007. During training, we parse passwords from the RockYou dataset and generate various rules and components. In the process, we populate our input dictionary with the frequencies of occurrences of each rule and component.

After this training phase, we obtain three *trained dictionaries* containing the component/rule and the corresponding frequency of occurrence. These include a dictionary of words, a dictionary of numerals, and a dictionary of characters and symbols. Upon breaking down a password into the components and rules, the score calculator makes a search count for the components and rules in the *trained dictionaries*. Using these values, a score corresponding to the input password is calculated using the scoring algorithm.

Characteristics of Password Collections

After deriving a model by training the system with a large number of passwords, this model can be used to assess the strength of passwords. We test this by computing password scores from five datasets, each one of which corresponds to a collection of passwords. Each dataset has different characteristics, as will be shown, which influences the average strength of the passwords and hence, the password scores. We first describe three major characteristics of all datasets.

The first obvious characteristic is the *type of resource being protected*, i.e., what would be lost if a password is stolen. We consider only the losses as perceived by the user who produces the password, and not those potentially suffered by other users as a result of theft or the losses of the organization associated with the password. The rationale is this: users are influenced by the risk they associate with theft when they select their password. For financial service providers, money would be lost. For social networking sites, the user would lose face or be inconvenienced. For a porn site, the loss may be limited to the access to the site. In addition to this, some private information, such as user name and address, may be at stake for all of these types of sites.

A second characteristic is the *demographics of users*. While it is not known how demographics affect password strength, it appears likely that they do.

Finally, the *collection method* could introduce a bias in the dataset. For example, if a dataset is obtained by malware attacks, the dataset may have a greater percentage of passwords from people who are not security conscious than if it was obtained by site corruption. Similarly, a dataset associated with phishing is likely to have a greater percentage of passwords from people who are gullible than other datasets would.

In the following, we will describe results associated with five datasets. The first dataset, the *Rootkit dataset* contains 64498 passwords. It was obtained by a compromise of rootkit.com. This website has forums about discussions of advanced topics in computer security. The demographics introduce a bias as relative to an average user, as most people registering on this website are more aware about security issues than typical users. Second, the *Paypal dataset* contains 19053 passwords. Most of the users behind the passwords are adults. The method of collection is phishing, which introduces a bias towards people who are more gullible. Third, the *Justin Bieber dataset* contains 5091 passwords and was obtained by a compromise of a fan website. Hence, there is no bias due to the collection method. However, the demographics introduce a bias as most of the users are teenagers. The fourth dataset is the *Sony dataset*, which contains 17785 passwords, and was obtained by a compromise of Sony Pictures Europe. As a result, there was no bias among passwords due to the collection method. And finally, the *Porn dataset* contains 8089 passwords, and was obtained by a compromise of a pornographic website. As a result, there is no bias due to the collection method. However, there is a visible bias associated with the type of resource being protected.

Training

Once we have decided with the input dictionary and the training dataset, which in our case is the RockYou dataset, we proceed to the training phase. Since, the dataset is huge, containing a total of 32 million passwords, it is first arranged as a tuple *(password, count)*. In this manner, passwords can be parsed quicker. Then the parser parses the dataset and creates three *trained dictionaries*. As mentioned earlier, three different trained dictionaries – a dictionary of words, a dictionary of characters and special symbols and a dictionary of numerals – are obtained after training on the dataset. The main reason to create three different populated dictionaries than one is that at the time of calculating the scores, the components may have a little overlap. For example, while parsing a password like "Spassword," it is better to first look for words rather than individual characters and hence, the word "password" should be parsed first followed by individual characters in order to obtain *maximum coverage*. Similarly, in the case of a password like "passw0rd," words should be parsed before numerals. Then it would be possible to detect L33T and hence, the word "password" with larger coverage could be obtained as compared to the word "pass" with smaller coverage. Thus, parsing will be more efficient if three different dictionaries are maintained against one.

2.5 Scoring Passwords

Scoring of passwords is straightforward once we have a parser and a list of frequencies of components and rules. We simply parse an input password and determine the frequency of each component and rule. Multiplying all of these frequencies with each other gives us a measure of the likelihood of the password.

Results

In this subsection, we analyze the usage of various rules and components in datasets described above. Using these analysis, we can better analyze the perceived security risks associated with these websites. This may lead to a better understanding of user behavior regarding creation of passwords. For example, it maybe useful to answer questions like how people's password creation policies change when the security risks involved are changed, and hoow various factors like type of resource being protected and demographics may influence password creation policies. These analysis also provide clues to a better password strength checker. We begin by comparing the usage of various rules and components in the datasets and then move onto analysis of passwords in individual datasets.

The Frequencies of Components: Words

Word components form the core of a large percentage of passwords, as can be seen in figure 2.1. The average number of word components per password is directly related to the average strength of the password. The Justin Bieber dataset has the highest average number of word components per password, whereas the Porn dataset has the lowest. It is not surprising that the Porn dataset is associated with a low average password security – after all, the loss of a password does not cause any great damage to a user, except if the user employs the same password elsewhere. However, it is a bit surprising that the Justin Bieber dataset exhibits a greater password security than the Paypal dataset – after all, the protected resources for the former are simply a user profile on a fan site. The reason may be that the Justin Bieber passwords were corrupted at the site while the Paypal passwords were stolen from gullible users, who are likely to use lower quality passwords than more security-conscious users are. It may also be due to demographic differences. At the same time, it is important to recognize that average quality is not a measure of how vulnerable the most exposed users are. As a case in point, it can be seen that a small number of words in the Justin Bieber dataset were used to construct a much larger number of passwords than any other dataset – see figure 2.2 for an illustration of this. This has a negative contribution to the average strength of passwords and counters the higher usage of word components per password in the Justin Bieber dataset. This is quite evident from table 2.1, where the average product of frequencies of all components per password is not the highest in the Justin Bieber dataset as the usage of word components is highly skewed. This forms maybe the best argument for why one should parse passwords. By doing so, it is possible to block the use of the most vulnerable passwords.

Table 2.1 The *average security* i.e., the average product of component frequencies for the passwords. The values are as expected with the Porn dataset taking the lowest value. The only exception is the Sony dataset having the largest average product.

Dataset	Security
JB	17.52
Rootkit	15.09
Paypal	15.77
Sony	18.67
Porn	13.79

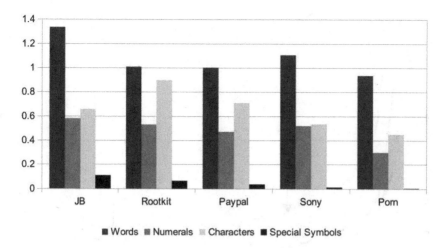

Fig. 2.1 The figure shows the average number of components per password in the different datasets.

The frequencies of components: Numerals

Common wisdom – expressed in the rules of password strength checkers – hold that it is good to include numerals in passwords. At the same time, it is clear that using numerals only make for weaker passwords. This is illustrated by figure 2.4, which visualizes a particular weakness of passwords in the Rootkit dataset: approximately 15% of all passwords in Rootkit dataset are numeric. If proposed passwords were decomposed as described herein, such weaknesses could easily be avoided. The use of numerals as components in passwords in general is illustrated in figure 2.1.

The frequencies of components: "Other"

The remaining components include leftover characters and special symbols obtained after "cutting" words and numerals from passwords. Even though usage of special symbols in passwords increases the effective size of the character set, special symbols are unpopular among users – see figure 2.1.

Even in the small percentage of special symbols which are used, the usage is highly skewed. Out of the 32 possible special symbols on standard ASCII keyboards, only a few of them have high frequencies. These special symbols are usually those which are used in rules like L33T – e.g., "@" and "&." Most of the remaining special symbols are rarely used. In fact, we found some special symbols which were almost never used in any of the datasets, such as "?" and "}." This is not a statistic anomaly given that the datasets contain over 100,000 passwords. It's a reminder that humans do not select passwords randomly, but rather, based on mnemonics and rules used by many others.

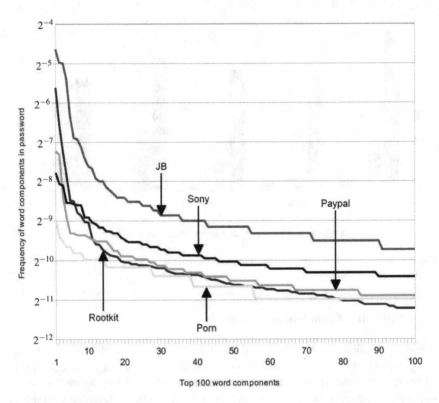

Fig. 2.2 The figure shows the frequencies of the top 100 most common words in each dataset. Even though passwords from the Justin Bieber dataset usually contain a larger number of components per password, it can be clearly seen that a small number of words are reused to a greater extent within that dataset.

The frequencies of rules: Concatenation

For a given password, the number of concatenation operations is one less than the total number of components. It can be clearly seen from figure 2.5 that concatenation is prevalent in all datasets. In fact, concatenation is the most used basic operation in all of the datasets. In the Justin Bieber dataset, it is as high as 1.67 concatenations, i.e., an average of 1.67 components per password. The higher usage of concatenation associated with higher security sites also indicates how people increase password security.

The Frequencies of Rules: L33T

Usage of L33T requires users to remember a new pattern replacing an old pattern which may require some effort, but can dramatically increase the strength of the

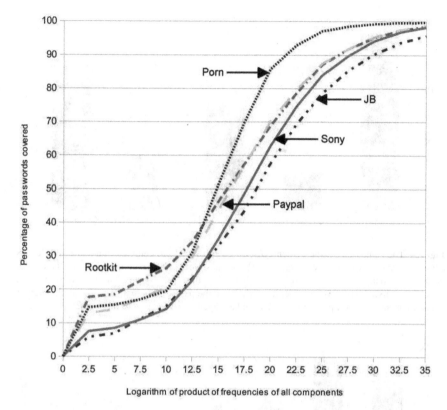

Fig. 2.3 The figure plots the cumulative distribution of the product of frequencies of all components of the passwords. This product is an estimate of the bit strength of the passwords. The Porn dataset stands out as having weaker passwords than the other datasets. By decomposing passwords into components and applying rules for minimum strength, it is possible to avoid weak passwords.

password. The average number of L33T operations per password is shown in figure 2.5. The highest value is for the Rootkits dataset, which supports our belief that there are demographic differences between password datasets, and that in particular, "geeks" are more frequent users of L33T than others.

Considering the scoring, if we were to assign a greater weight to using L33T than concatenation, we could "reward" users who use uncommon rules.

The Frequencies of Rules: Spelling Mistakes

The usage of spelling mistakes is quite interesting. To begin with, it is not possible for us to determine whether spelling mistakes are intentional or not, whereas the use of other rules are evidently intentional. Unintentional spelling mistakes, in the context of password strength, is therefore an excellent example of a case where ig-

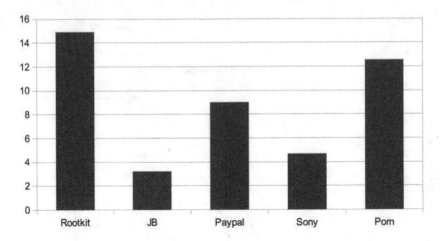

Fig. 2.4 The figure shows the percentage of passwords that are complete numerals. While this contradicts the current password rules of Paypal passwords, where complete numerals are not permitted – many of the captured passwords predate this rule. By applying password strength assessments like the one we propose, not only when the password is first created, but also during login, weak and non-compliant passwords can be tagged and users be asked to update passwords.

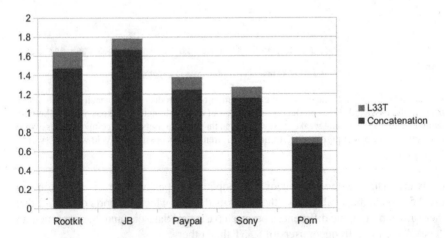

Fig. 2.5 The average use of concatenation and L33T rules per password for different datasets. L33T (pronounced "leet") is the replacement of characters with similar-looking characters – for example, making "@ppl3" from "apple."

norance is bliss. Figure 2.6 shows the prevalence of spelling mistakes in the different datasets with much greater frequency in the Porn dataset.

While the different datasets exhibit different rates of spelling errors, they are all relatively low in comparison to other rules. The low frequency of the use of spelling mistakes emphasizes the potential value of this rule to password security.

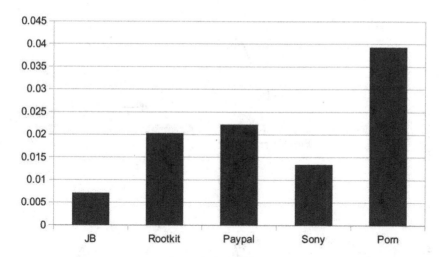

Fig. 2.6 The average number of spelling mistakes per password for the different datasets. The use of this rule is dramatically less common than both L33T and concatenation.

Score Calculation.

The score calculator we describe here uses only the frequencies of rules and components, not the location or order of them. The score calculator utilizes the three different trained dictionaries of words, characters and special symbols, and numerals. All of these are obtained by training on the RockYou dataset.

The frequencies are measured by dividing the count of occurrences by the total count. The score calculator utilizes the frequencies of rule occurrences in that dataset. These are obtained by analysis of passwords of each particular dataset. The score of a password is simply calculated by multiplying the frequencies of all the rules and components occurring in the password. Since all frequencies are between 0 and 1, the score will also be a small value in range of 0 and 1. The second logarithm of this product is an assessment of the bit strength of a password.

Comparison of Scores.

Figure 2.7 shows the distribution of password scores for the passwords of the different datasets. Note the close resemblance to a bell curve. Password crackers target the most frequent credentials, corresponding to the passwords with the lowest scores. The clearly insecure region from figure 2.7 is magnified in figure 2.8. The cumulative distribution of password scores is shown in figure 2.9.

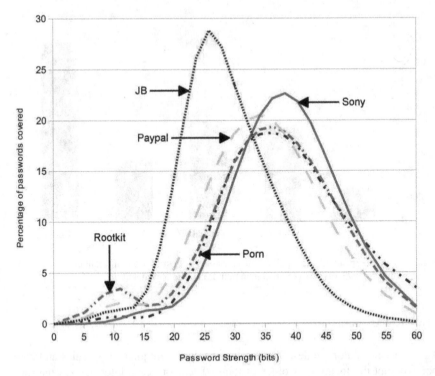

Fig. 2.7 The figure shows the distribution of password strengths as assessed by multiplying the frequencies of rules and components used. The second logarithm of these values correspond to the bit strength of the passwords. It is evident that passwords from the Porn dataset are weaker than the passwords of the other datasets.

2.6 Identifying Similarity

One of the big vulnerabilities associated with typical password use is the common reuse of passwords across multiple sites. Users have accounts on various websites and each website requires them to remember a username, password combination for authentication. As the number of accounts increases, it becomes quite difficult for a user to remember all her passwords. Hence, people reuse passwords. Password reuse is usually not a good idea as different websites have different security threats related to them. A phisher who compromises the password of an email account has a very good chance of being able to access the financial accounts of the same user, provided he can determine the user name used for those. (This may be evident from scanning the mailbox from emails from financial service providers.) At the same time, the understanding of the degree of password reuse is very poor to date. We offer a glimpse at the magnitude of this problem in this section.

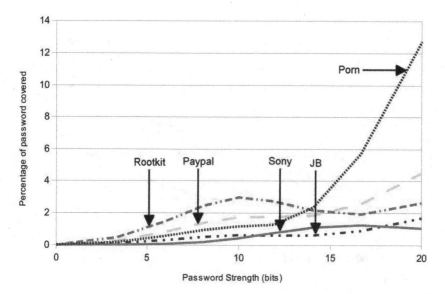

Fig. 2.8 This figure shows a portion of the graph in figure 2.7. This portion of the distribution corresponds to unnecessarily weak passwords. By decomposing passwords and scoring them in the manner we describe, such passwords can be avoided.

An average user has 6.5 passwords, each of which is shared across 3.9 different websites [28]. A user with 25 accounts therefore only remembers the 6 or 7 basic passwords he or she uses, and what password is used where.

Small modifications to existent passwords are also used to generate new passwords. One of the ways in which users tackle the problem of remembering a large number of passwords for their different accounts is by crafting interrelated or similar passwords. A base password is used and then reused with slight modifications to generate passwords for other websites – and to comply with differing password rules. Therefore, even though different accounts owned by one user may not share the same password, the passwords can be quite similar to each other. Fraudsters know this and are likely to try common variations of passwords they steal. For example, a user may choose a base password, 'password' and generate new passwords like 'password123' (numeral concatenation), 'passwordabc' (concatenation), 'Password' (capitalization), 'passw0rd' (L33T), and so forth. Thus, users generally introduce new components or rules, or modify existing components in order to generate new passwords. (Sadly, these are real examples of passwords and not all too uncommon.)

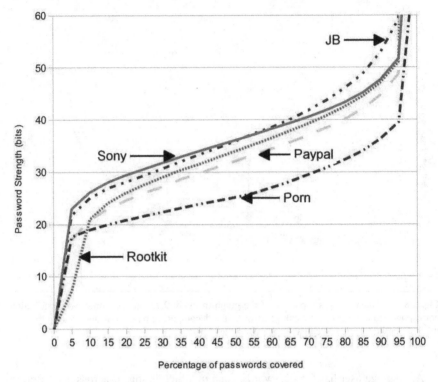

Fig. 2.9 The figure shows the cumulative distribution of password strengths as assessed by multiplying the frequencies of rules and components used. The second logarithm of these values correspond to the bit strength of the passwords.

Dataset

In our analysis, we identify verbatim as well as approximate password reuse, using a dataset obtained by Paypal from a security vendor. The passwords were stolen by a malware, most likely using a key logger that was triggered by the establishment of SSL, or interaction with a password field. These stolen passwords were stored in a dropbox, as commonly done by fraudsters, which in turn was raided by the security vendor to determine what accounts to flag. The dataset contains over 11,000 passwords stolen from 3,550 users, corresponding to an average of 3.174 passwords per user.

Similarity of passwords.

Table 2.2 shows the extent of password reuse. For users for whom only two passwords were compromised, for example, these two passwords were identical for 17% of the users. Similarly, for users for whom three passwords were compromised, at

Table 2.2 The table shows the probability of identifying password reuse between at least two passwords, provided a varying number of observed passwords of a user.

Number of passwords available	Two Passwords are same
Two passwords	17%
Three passwords	36%
Four passwords	71%
Five passwords	85%
Six or more passwords	100%

least two passwords were identical in 36% of the cases. When we get to users for whom six or more passwords were compromised, we see a 100It is evident that password reuse is rampant!

Table 2.3 The table shows the average *Levenshtein distance* of password pairs. As the Levenshtein distance increases, the percentage of passwords having Levenshtein distance decreases. This means that most people who use similar but not identical passwords at different sites make relatively small changes when producing new passwords.

Levenshtein distance	Percentage of Passwords
L 1	5.81%
L 2	5.14%
L 3	2.78%
L 4	2.72%
L 5	2.24%

Table 2.4 Variation of Hamming distance with number of passwords. Unlike Levenshtein distance, the percentage of passwords decreases until HM 3, then increases. We believe that this is directly influenced by the similar structure of many English words. This also suggests that Levenshtein distance may be a better measure to calculate password similarity than Hamming distance.

Hamming Distance	Percentage of Passwords
HM 1	3.93%
HM 2	1.51%
HM 3	1.27%
HM 4	2.84%
HM 5	5.99%

However, this table is not a true reflection of extent of password reuse as it doesn't include those passwords which are similar but not identical. We determined that passwords not identical had high levels of similarity. This was done by computing the *Hamming distance* and *Levenshtein distance* of pairs of passwords of the same user. The Levenshtein distance between two strings is a basic edit distance function that corresponds to the minimum edit distance that transforms a first string into a second string, where the number of deletions, insertions, and substitutions are counted. The Hamming distance is defined as the number of characters which differ between two strings, i.e. the number of characters which need to be changed to turn one string into the other. We refer to tables 2.3 and 2.4 for our observations.

If the Levenshtein distance is less than or equal to four, there is a strong similarity of passwords. This was manually verified as well: the passwords with low Levenshtein distance were confirmed to be derivations of each other. This manual analysis identified that common techniques used to derive passwords from each other were capitalization, L33T, and numeral concatenation.

Chapter 3
Your Password is Your New PIN

Markus Jakobsson, Debin Liu

Abstract

This chapter will describe a method of deriving new PINs from existing passwords. This method is useful for obtaining friction-free user onboarding to mobile platforms. It has significant business benefits for organizations that wish to introduce mobile apps to existing users who already have passwords, but are reluctant to authenticate the users with the existing passwords. From the user's perspective, a PIN is easier to enter than a password, and a *derived* PIN does not need to be remembered – assuming the user has a password and can recall it. In addition, even though the PINs are derived from passwords, they do not contain sufficient information to make the passwords easy to infer from compromised PINs. This, along with different transaction limits for PINs and passwords, makes the derived PINs more useful in a situation where users have to enter their PINs in public. We describe real-life password distributions to quantify exactly how much information about the passwords the derived PINs contain, and how much information is *lost* during the derivation. We also describe experiments with human subjects to qualitatively and quantitatively show that the user-side derivation method is easy to use.

3.1 PINs and Friction

It has been shown that users do not like passwords, especially if they have to enter their passwords on mobile handsets [46]: Password entry on handsets is found to be more annoying than lack of coverage, small screen size, or poor voice quality. It has also been shown (see chapter 4) that the time to enter a typical strong password takes 2-3 times longer on a mobile handset than on a regular keyboard.

As a result of user preferences, there is an industry trend towards using PINs instead of passwords on handsets, gaming consoles, store checkouts, and other appliances with similar constraints and security profiles. For example, many smartphone apps ask for a PIN instead of a password to authenticate users.

Although PINs offer improved convenience to users, service providers are hesitant to request users with pre-existing passwords to also create PINs. From a business standpoint, *any* increase of the end-user friction is worrisome. Having to force millions of existing users to create PINs is not desirable at all. Moreover, users tend to create PINs that are easy for them to remember, which often makes them weak.

M. Jakobsson, *Mobile Authentication*, SpringerBriefs in Computer Science,
DOI: 10.1007/978-1-4614-4878-5_3, © The Author(s) 2013

For example, approximately one in five users selects their PINs as their birthdate [7]. This not only means that database-scraping attackers have an edge, but also leads to a restricted distribution of PINs, given there are only 365 days in a year. It is also well understood that people commonly reuse PINs, just as they reuse passwords (as discussed in chapter 2). This means that if one PIN is compromised, then that may put other accounts at risk as well. For those who do not use any of these tricks to remember PINs, it is relatively common to *forget* them: Roughly one in ten report having forgotten a PIN [7]. Forrester research [17] estimates the average costs of a help desk assisted reset at $70 per request, making forgotten credentials a commercially very expensive security problem. (Also see chapter 5 for a discussion of credential resets).

In this chapter, we will describe a method that *bootstraps* the generation of PINs to create an automated onboarding of an overwhelming majority of users. This is achieved by deriving PINs from already established passwords – without explicit user involvement. The user would, in fact, not even be aware of the PIN creation until she is told that she *has* a PIN, and should use it to log in. A four-digit PIN is set as the first four characters of the password, mapped to a numeric keypad[1]. In principle, this mapping from passwords to PINs is analogous to how alphanumeric phone numbers are mapped to a 10-button keypad – like 1-800 CALL ATT *becomes* 1-800 225 5288. Similarly, the password "Blu2thrules" becomes the PIN "2582", since "B" maps to "2", "l" maps to "5", "u" maps to "8", and "2" maps to "2".

We will show how much information a derived PIN reveals about the underlying password. This is relevant to consider in order to understand the consequences of a derived PIN being compromised. We also show that derived PINs have approximately the same *entropy* as traditional user-created PINs do. Therefore, this method does not result in weaker PINs. The security analysis is based on millions of real-life passwords and the PINs derived from those passwords.

3.2 How to Derive PINs from Passwords

This section describes in detail how to derive PINs from existing passwords. This is done on the backend without any active user involvement.

Derivation Approach. Passwords are commonly stored on the backend as the output of a hash function along with a salt. It is not possible to derive PINs from salted and hashed passwords. *However*, it is possible to derive PINs from passwords when the passwords are temporarily available in plaintext – as they are each time a user logs in. Therefore, we can bootstrap the derived PIN from the plaintext password once it has been verified to be correct – but before it is erased.

---

[1] In this chapter, we will always think of PINs as four-digit elements. It is straightforward to modify our techniques to derive six-digit PINs. However, while this leads to a reduced risk of PINs being guessed, the amount of information in the PIN about the associated password increases. This has negative effects in situations where PINs are compromised.

Fig. 3.1 The figure shows the user interface of what she would see after tapping on the PIN window. To log in, the user would simply enter the first four characters of her password, using the numeric keypad. If a password character is "2," "A," "a," "B," "b," "C," or "c," then the user presses the 2-button. A password starting with "Blu2" would correspond to the PIN "2852."

Storage of Derived PINs. On the backend, each of the derived PINs are salted and hashed before they are stored. This hardens the file of stored PINs against compromised. It does not provide the same degree of protection as salting and hashing of passwords do – due to the lower credential entropy – but this is a problem that is inherent to PINs and not specific to *derived* PINs.

The User Perspective. Users would not need to know that PINs are derived from their passwords. It will happen without their knowledge as they authenticate to the system using their password. When a user for whom a PIN has been derived arrives to the mobile authentication interface (or any other PIN authentication interface), she would be told that, "She has a PIN," and given an instruction of how to derive it from her password. As a result, users do not have to remember their PINs – it is enough to remember the passwords. A screenshot of a possible user interface is shown in figure 3.1.

Messaging. The backend "knows" for which users PINs have been derived, and messages those users when they arrive at a mobile portal (or another portal where PIN entry is preferred by the system). The messages must be clear and instructive, and also short and concise to account for the limited screen size, and to avoid being ignored. One possible approach is simply to state, "Your PIN is the first four characters of your password. Please enter your PIN."

Managing Special Cases. There are several rare cases in which the PIN derivation approach cannot be applied directly.

1. **How to deal with unmappable characters?**
   An unmappable character is a character that is not on a typical numeric keypad. For example, there is not a number on a numeric keypad that can be used to map

a dollar sign. The frequency of passwords containing unmappable characters is marginal – less than 2.6% on average in our data samples. Simply speaking, this special case can be addressed in at least two ways: (a) one can map all special characters to one digit (e.g., "0"), or (b) one can simply "disqualify" passwords containing unmappable characters among the first four characters. The latter would force the owner of such a password to manually create a PIN – in the old-fashioned way – or update his/her password. One approach to increase automatic enrollment is to augment password strength checkers to reject unmappable characters in the first four positions of passwords that are created. Given the very low rates of unmappable characters in the first four positions, this has no practical impact on the security of the passwords.

2. **What if a strong password becomes a weak PIN?**
   A password is considered *strong* if it is sufficiently uncommon – otherwise *weak*. Similarly, some PINs are so commonly used that they are considered weak. For example, "1234" is one such PIN. There is a case that strong passwords result in weak PINs. An example is a strong password such as "1234GreyFrieS#" and the associated weak derived PIN "1234."
   To avoid weak derived PINs, we could reject the corresponding password (as is commonly the policy); accept the password but not derive a PIN; or derive a PIN but demand that it be updated on its first use. The approach taken is a matter of security policy for service providers.

3. **What if users change their passwords?**
   If a PIN is derived from a password, and then used for some time, then the user may either think of the PIN in terms of the password it is derived from or she may have learned the PIN. In the latter case, the PIN would become independent of the password in the mind of the user. The backend cannot know whether this has happened or not. Therefore, if the user were to change her password, the backend could create two "parallel universes" – with the *old* derived PIN and the *new* derived PIN. Both are valid until one of them is used, at which point the other one is erased.

4. **How to derive PINs for hardware keyboards?**
   Some mobile handsets, like some old BlackBerries, have hardware keyboards. When the user is asked to enter her password, the hardware keyboard would be momentarily shut off, and the PIN entry would be performed using the touchscreen keyboard. But some old BlackBerries do not have touch screens either. Since apps are platform aware (if not platform specific), apps on non-compliant platforms would simply not offer users an option to log in using a derived PIN, but would require them to create a PIN out of hand – as is currently required for *all* users.
   Other handsets, such as the typical phone from the mid-2000s, have hardware keyboards with the proper mapping; however, people are used to pressing each button one or more times in a row to advance to the right character. This can be detected and compensated for on the backend, or the user can be instructed to only press each button once for each character.

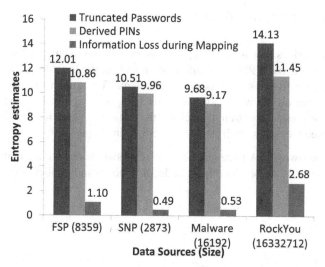

Fig. 3.2 The figure shows entropy estimates for the truncated passwords, e corresponding derived PINs; and the information loss during the mapping process from passwords to PINs. The numbers are different for the four groups of passwords – primarily, the estimates are different due to the impact of different sample sizes, as shown in figure 3.3. Moreover, they are *inherently* different, most likely due to differing rules governing password acceptance and different security mentalities among end users. The first two groups correspond to phishing dropboxes for our FSP (Financial Service Provider) and SNP (Social Networking Provider), the third group corresponds to a malware dropbox containing credentials to any domain that was accessed from the infected machines, and the fourth group corresponds to the public exposed RockYou passwords.

A *dropbox* is a file created and used by hackers to temporarily store stolen credentials. Many financial organizations and security vendors attempt to raid dropboxes – i.e., locate them and copy their contents. This is done to restrict access to compromised accounts. Some dropboxes were used by phishers, others by malware authors. One difference is that on rare occasion, would-be victims of phishing attacks are aware of being targeted and instead of entering their real credentials, enter insults. This is not the case for malware dropboxes where victims are more "sincere." Another difference is that phishing drop-boxes typically only have credentials for one particular site (the spoofed site), whereas malware dropboxes contain any credential that the malware agent could obtain. Also, naive users fall for phishing, whereas malware is a prob-lem of poor computer security hygiene, which may be the result of another person's decisions.

3.3 Analysis of Passwords and Derived PINs

This section describes how to use real password collections to analyze the information contained in derived PINs and information lost during the derivation process. The measure of entropy is used as a way of quantifying strength in this section, and to permit the use of well-known notions such as conditional entropy. Other approaches for measuring strength include the notion of *guesswork* [72, 9] and frequency-based measures, such as those described in chapter 2.

The studied passwords. A large number of real passwords are studied in this chapter. These passwords are obtained from raided dropboxes and publicly exposed credentials.

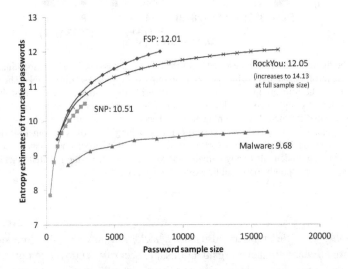

Fig. 3.3 The figure shows a strong dependency on the sample size of the truncated passwords from the four data sources. True entropies are at least as great as estimates for the 100% sample measurements, but extrapolation of these curves suggest that still bigger sample sizes would most likely have shown yet higher estimates of source entropies.

Passwords from four sources are studied: (1) Phished credentials corresponding to a major financial service provider (8359 passwords); (2) Phished credentials corresponding to a major social networking provider (2873 passwords); (3) passwords stolen by malware, corresponding to a variety of service providers (16192 passwords); and (4) passwords exposed in the corruption of the RockYou[2] site (16332712 passwords). We refer to these sources as FSP (financial service provider), SNP (social networking provider), malware, and RockYou.

---

[2] The RockYou passwords were exposed in December 2009 in the breach of social media application developer website (www.rockyou.com) [61]. Before that, there has never been such a high volume of exposed real-world passwords.

The passwords from different groups have different distributions. This can be determined using the Kolmogorov-Smirnov test or the Wilcoxon Rand Sum test. The difference in distribution may be attributed to different rules for what qualifies as a good password on various domains, and to differing user security mentalities for the three different types of domains (see chapter 2).

Computing the entropy of derived PINs. To estimate the entropy of the derived PINs from the passwords of each group (corresponding to the four groups described above), one would first truncate the passwords to the first four characters resulting in what can be referred to as pwd_4. Then one would count – within each group of passwords – the relative frequencies of each value of pwd_4. For example, the password "Blu2thrules" would be truncated to become $pwd_4 =$ "Blu2," and a counter for this very string would be increased. After that, given the relative frequencies, the entropies [87] of the first four characters of the passwords from different groups would be computed.

There are at least $26^4 \approx 457000$ possible four-character combinations without taking case, numerical values or special characters into consideration. In contrast, the first three groups have between 2000 and 17000 passwords for each group, which causes a rather low density of occurrences. This, in turn, results in complete lack of observation of some combinations that may occur in larger password populations and a slightly inaccurate estimate for the frequencies in general. As a result, it is clear that one will underestimate the associated entropies when using small sample sizes. The impact of the sample size on the entropy estimate is shown in figure 3.3. The larger password set allows us to anticipate the real entropy from the sources corresponding to the smaller datasets.

Numeric mapping is then performed for all truncated passwords pwd_4. For example, this would map the pwd_4 string "Blu2" to "2582," using the mapping resulting from the common interface shown in figure 3.1. As a result, there are exactly 10000 possible mapped strings. For each of these, the relative frequency is determined, given the mapped and truncated passwords from the four data groups. Like the entropy assessments from the unmapped passwords, the entropy assessments of the mapped passwords will be slight underestimates (but closer to the truth given that the mapping increased the distribution density).

Password and PIN Entropy Estimates. Figure 3.2 shows the entropy estimates of the first four characters of *unmapped* passwords and the derived PINs – i.e., the *mapped* and truncated passwords. It also shows the information loss during the mapping process.

It is notable that sample sizes play a substantial role when producing entropy estimates – especially for the unmapped samples, where the density is sparser than for the mapped samples. To determine the effects of this, one can randomly sample the first three data sources (the FSP, the SNP, and the malware groups whose sizes have a similar order of magnitude) from 10% to 100% of their original size. Then, we downsample the RockYou passwords to similar sizes. The entropies of the truncated passwords and derived PINs for every sample are then estimated, and compared to the entropy estimates for the full RockYou collection.

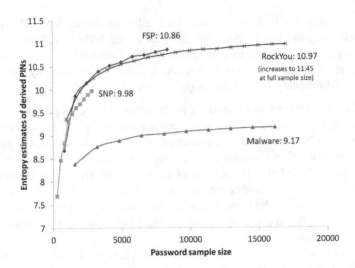

Fig. 3.4 The figure shows the dependency on sample size for entropy estimates of derived PINs for all four data sources. The differences in estimated entropies are slightly smaller than for the truncated passwords (figure 3.3), as the derived PINs have a denser distribution than the truncated passwords do.

Figure 3.3 shows a strong dependency on the sample size when estimating the entropy of truncated passwords. Figure 3.4 shows a similar dependency when estimating the entropy of derived PINs. Both dependencies are due to the fact that low densities of samples create an artificially low estimate of the entropy, given how entropies are estimated. This analysis suggests that bigger sample sizes are likely to further increase entropy estimates. They also suggest one can improve the situation by using the large collection of RockYou passwords to extrapolate the estimates of the true entropy of the FSP, the SNP, and the malware groups.

If we wish to estimate the true entropy of the FSP group, for example, we can sample down the RockYou passwords to the size of the FSP passwords (8359 samples) and compare the two estimates. We obtain an entropy estimate of 11.64 for the truncated passwords and 10.77 for the associated derived PINs for the downsampled RockYou collection. This is less than the corresponding entropy estimates for FSP. From this, we can conclude that actual FSP entropies are likely to be at least as big as those for the full RockYou samples.

Estimated entropy of the first four characters of the RockYou passwords is 14.13 for truncated passwords and 11.45 for derived PINs. This corresponds to an increase of 21% in the entropy estimate for the truncated passwords over the downsampled version of the same dataset, and 6% for the associated derived PIN set. (Note that the underestimate was greater for the sparser set.)

Using these values, we can extrapolate entropies for the FSP passwords – both four character prefixes and derived PINs – giving us an extrapolated entropy estimates of 14.58 for the truncated FSP passwords (an increase of 21% from the original entropy estimate of 12.01) and 11.55 for the corresponding derived PINs (an increase of 6% from the original entropy estimate, 10.86). Better estimates can be obtained by more careful modeling.

Figure 3.5 shows the extrapolated entropies of the truncated passwords and the corresponding derived PINs for the FSP, SNP, and malware data sources. In addition, the maximum entropy ($log_2(10000)$) a 4-digit PIN can have and the entropy estimate of a 4-digit user-generated PIN based on our experiment (details in section 3.5) are presented for comparison.

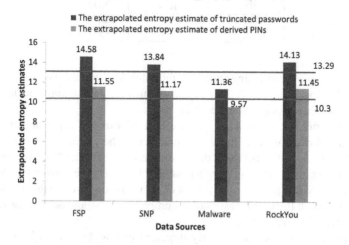

Fig. 3.5 The figure shows the extrapolated entropy estimates of the truncated passwords and the extrapolated entropies of the corresponding derived PINs for the FSP, SNP, and malware data groups. For purposes of comparison, it also shows the maximum entropy of 4-digit PINs (upper line) and an entropy estimate of traditional 4-digit PINs (lower line).

The use of special characters. Since special characters in a password affects the derivation of PINs, it is important to estimate how common they are. It turns out that among the four password groups we studied, less than 2.6% had a non-alphanumeric character among the first four characters. The frequency with which one or more of the first four characters is "unmappable" is 1.44% (FSP), 1.95% (SNP), 6.16% (malware), and 0.64% (RockYou).

3.4 Security Analysis

This section will examine the security of the derived PINs.

Security Impact of Compromise. According to entropy estimates of the RockYou password group, an adversary can gain 11.45 bits of information about a password if he compromises the corresponding derived PIN. The mapping itself destroyed 2.68 bits of information and truncated the rest. Here, the exact amount of information lost by truncation depends on the length of the password. Table 3.1 presents the length of an average password from each password group. The average password length among all the passwords is roughly 9 characters, which according to NIST's entropy estimates [67] corresponds to an entropy of 19.5 bits.

Table 3.1 How long is an average password?

Password Group	Password Length	Sample Size
FSP	8.8	8359
SNP	10.4	2873
Malware	7.6	16192
RockYou	9.4	16332712

Using the sample estimating approach, the entropy of the entire untruncated passwords in the RockYou group is 21.47. This number suggests that the actual entropy is a bit higher than was estimated by NIST [67].

In a scenario that an attacker gets the derived PIN, he can learn on average 11.45 bits information from the whole password. There is a *conditional entropy* of $21.47 - 11.45 \simeq 10$ bits (using the entropy estimate for the RockYou password set) corresponding to the security of a password for which the derived PIN has been compromised. While this is not terrific, it ought to be compared to the much starker situation in which the entire password is compromised, when used on insecure devices instead of derived PINs.

Moreover, one can set up an early detection of possible credential leaking by looking for a combination of a successful login with derived PIN and a failed password login attempt. This type of observation suggests that the derived PIN must have leaked and that the user should be authenticated using alternative means, and asked to create either a new PIN or a new password (from which a new PIN can be derived).

Comparing Derived PINs and Traditional PINs. The entropies of derived PINs were 11.55 (FSP), 11.17 (SNP), 9.57 (Malware), and 11.45 (RockYou) using extrapolated entropy estimates. This should be compared to the general estimates of the entropy of PINs that are *not* derived from passwords. Section 3.5 will show that the traditional user selected 4-digit PINs have an entropy of approximately 10.8 bits based on a human subjects experiment. Although the number 10.8 is not a perfect estimate, it is an indication that the derived PINs are not weaker – given their estimated entropy of 10.9 for the password distributions we described. There is, however, anecdotal evidence suggesting that the lower quartile of derived PINs is notably more secure than the lower quartile of traditional PINs. This is due to the lack of very common combinations for derived PINs, and the relatively common use of years and dates as traditional PINs. Moreover, if the (beginning of the) password is not reused, then the derived PIN is independent of other PINs created from other related passwords.

3.5 How do people select their PINs?

There are strong indications that PINs are selected in a way that inherently causes weaker credentials than other alternatives do. Most people use only one strategy to create PINs, and most of the strategies inherently result in reuse of information, much of which is potentially public.

To understand how people select their PINs, 200 subjects were recruited on Amazon Mechanical Turk. Each of them was paid $0.29. Most of them follow one out of a small number of common mental generation rules to select PINs. The observed PIN selection rules are listed below.

1. **Date - "My PIN uses a date when some special event occurred."**
   This is the most popular rule people use to create their PINs. 26% of the participants say they use somebody's birthday or a date they always remember for some reasons. There are, of course, only 365 days in a year, which is much less than what can be expressed using a 4-digit PIN. Similar findings are reported in [11] that 23% of users use dates as their PIN selection method.
2. **Year - "My PIN uses a year during which something special happened."**
   This is the second most popular PIN generation rule. 22% of the participants use a year as their PIN. It might be the year someone was born. Or, as one participant said, "I normally use the year that my favorite movie came out. Say the movie *Hackers* came out in 1995. Then my PIN would be 1995." People typically choose years during which they were alive, which is far less than what can be expressed using four digits.
3. **Something Familiar/School ID/SSN/Phone Number - "My PIN is part of something I know."**
   A lot of people create their PINs by connecting their PINs with something they are familiar with and thus always remember. 19% of the participants use part of a phone number; 9% of them use part of an address; 9% of them use their SSN; 2% of them use their school or company ID; and 5% of them use part of some other number they remember for other reasons. For example, one participant said, "The truck I drive for work is numbered. I use some of the numbers from the truck as my PIN."
4. **Spell Out Letters - "My PIN spells out the first four letters of something I remembers."**
   (16%) of participants chose their PINs to spell out the first four letters of their hometown or someone's name. For example, one participant said, "I use my son's name, Matt, by choosing the corresponding numbers on a keypad."
5. **Random Number - "I use random numbers as my PIN."**
   11% of the participants say they use random numbers as their PINs. Apparently, they do have very good memory to remember this - or the number may not be as random as claimed.

6. **Default PIN - "I don't change PINs. My PIN is always the default set by the providers."**

   10% of the participants never change their default PINs! One participant said, "I just remember them. All of the PINs I have were generated by the providers." Indeed, many default PINs are easy to remember, and also easy to guess.

7. **Keypad Pattern - "My PIN maps the pattern on my keypad."**

   9% of the participants reported that they use the patterns on the keypad to create their PINs. This is corroborated by a large-scale study of actual iPhone passwords by app developer Daniel Amitay, who found that the ten most common PINs (all obvious patterns on the keypad) account for 14% of all PINs [7]. For example, the PIN "2580" (a vertical line on a numeric keypad) is chosen by a little more than 4% of users.

The number of responses and percentages for each PIN-generation method are first counted. The estimates of the entropies of a 4-digit PIN using other PIN-generation methods are then computed. These are *upper bounds* without knowing the distributions within each type, and therefore assuming uniform distribution gives a higher entropy estimate than will actually occur.

Table 3.2 How to choose PINs?

Method	Percentage	Entropy
Using Years	22%	6.6
Using Dates	26%	8.5
Spell Out Letters	16%	10
Keypad Mapping	9%	4.32
Others	87%	13.3

For simplicity, assuming people can randomly choose a year between 1900 and 2010 as their PINs would give an entropy estimate of $E_1 = log_2(110) = 6.6$ using the entropy definition for any PIN chosen as a year. Assuming there are 365 days a year and people can randomly choose a month and a date to create a 4-digit PIN would give an entropy estimate of $E_2 = log_2(12 \times 30) = 8.5$. According to 4.6, a 4-digit PIN mapped from a password has an entropy estimate of $E_3 = 10$. This is based on the approximation that the mnemonics that are mapped will have a similar distribution as passwords. Assuming there are 20 factory default PINs and they are evenly distributed would give an estimate of an entropy of $E_4 = log_2(1/20) = 4.32$. In addition, assuming all the other PINs which are not generated by years, dates, or keypad mapping as *uniformly random* PINs would give an upper bound on the entropy of $E_5 = 4 \times log_2(10) = 13.3$.

The percentages and entropy estimates are presented in table 3.2.

The weighted average entropy of a 4-digit user-selected PIN is approximately 10.8. 4.6 shows a 4-digit PIN derived from a password has an entropy value of 10.9, which suggests that derived PINs do not reduce security.

Chapter 4
Like Passwords – But Faster, Easier and More Secure

Markus Jakobsson, Ruj Akavipat

Abstract

We describe and analyze a variant of the traditional password scheme. This is designed to take advantage of standard error-correcting methods used to facilitate text entry on handsets. We call the new approach *fastwords* to emphasize their primary regular passwords; the former being. Fastwords are approximately twice as fast to enter on mobile keyboards, and three times as fast on full-size keyboards than regular passwords. This is supported by user studies reported herein. Furthermore, these user studies show that fastwords also have considerably greater entropy than passwords, and that their recall rates are dramatically higher than that of passwords and PINs.

The new structure permits a memory jogging technique in which a portion of the fastword is revealed to a user who has forgotten it. We show that this results in boosted recall rates, while maintaining a security above that of traditional passwords. We also introduce the notion of equivalence classes – whether based on semantics or pronunciation – and describe uses, including voice-based authentication. The new technology does not need any client-side modification.

4.1 Auto-Correction and Auto-Completion

Security protocols have developed at a pace largely matching the development of online threats, but password technology has remained the same, in spite of increasing pressure on authentication mechanisms [36]. Mobile authentication, in particular, poses new problems due to the limitations of handset keyboards [78].

Text entry on handsets is time-consuming and error-prone, hence, auto-correction and auto-completion methods are ubiquitous. However, auto-correction and auto-completion only work for *text* – not for password entry. This is due to the fact that good passwords are much like poorly spelled words, and error-correction techniques help *remove* poor spelling. While the dictionaries used by error-correction techniques can be augmented with words they should recognize, it is naturally not a good idea to augment them with passwords – even though it *would* help to enter them. Therefore, better error-correction techniques help maintain usability of text entry as we move towards smaller, feedback-free on-screen keyboards. However,

M. Jakobsson, *Mobile Authentication*, SpringerBriefs in Computer Science,
DOI: 10.1007/978-1-4614-4878-5_4, © The Author(s) 2013

they do *not* help us enter traditional passwords, which have become *harder* to input as a result. This is likely to give rise to increased reliance on password managers and short passwords – neither of which bode well for user security.

A recent study by Jakobsson et al. [47] reports that consumers find entering text and passwords on handsets only *slightly* less frustrating than slow web connections on such devices, and both to be much more frustrating than lack of coverage and poor voice quality. In a survey we performed, two in five users expressed annoyance with entering passwords on handsets, and one in five stated that they avoid situations that require them to enter passwords on handsets.

This chapter addresses the question of how to facilitate human-to-machine authentication on constrained input devices. To benefit from error-correction techniques, we need to permit dictionary words. At the heart of our solution is the insight that dictionary words are easy to enter if error-correction is enabled – and that a *sequence* of dictionary words becomes a secure credential. We refer to this as a *fastword*.

To make our proposal concrete, let's consider an example. As a user sets up an account or changes access credentials, he is offered the possibility of selecting a "mobile friendly" credential. Let's assume a participating user chooses the fastword "frog work flat," which might correspond to the mnemonic "I ran over a frog on my way to work, and now I have a flat frog under the tire."[1]

Our example system would accept the fastword "frog word flat" as a strong credential, given that the frequencies[2] of the three words in English language are $2^{-17.0}$, $2^{-10.6}$, and $2^{-14.5}$ (resulting in a *product* of frequencies of $2^{-42.3}$); and that the 3-gram frequency is $2^{-49.5}$. The latter is the frequency of the three words *together* in the English language. In contrast, the four-word fastword "I love you honey" might be rejected in spite of the fact that the product of word frequencies ($2^{-7.8}$, $2^{-11.8}$, $2^{-7.8}$, and $2^{-16.3}$) is $2^{-43.7}$, since the frequency of the 4-gram is only $2^{-25.8}$.

The frequency measures described above do not reflect how secure a credential is against an adversary who tries the k most common credentials, but how secure it is *on average*. However, by using a database of frequencies of keywords in previously registered fastwords – and not only considering their frequencies in the English language – the system can turn down fastwords that are starting to become too common, thereby avoiding the "most popular credential" attack. This is analogous to the work by Schechter et al. [81] in the context of traditional passwords.

We do not permit keywords to be selected as names[3], or many users may be tempted to select names of friends and family members – which are often possible to gather from social networks. It is possible to implement any such policies by simple changes on the backend; it is also much easier to enunciate the policies in

---

[1] Research into human memory suggests that colorful phrases are easier to recall than more mundane ones, but this is orthogonal to the work described herein.

[2] We use the Microsoft N-Gram Service to assess word frequencies; alternative services may result in slightly different estimates.

[3] Many names are not found in dictionaries; those that are can easily be excluded in an automated manner, given the labeling of words in common dictionaries. In Webster, for example, all names are labelled *biographical name*.

the context of our proposed solution than it is for traditional passwords since we can easily parse fastwords on a component level. Any fastword that is considered insufficiently strong will be refused; the user can either simply be told to enter a new one, or be told of the rule that caused the fastword to be rejected.

The proposed solution has three main benefits: (1) The *increased speed and convenience* it provides – measured in terms of the time it takes to enter a credential; (2) the *improved security* – both in terms of the average and minimum security; and (3) substantially *higher recall rates* than passwords and PINs. These rates are further boosted by the use of hints given to a user who has forgotten his or her fastword – for the fastword "frog work flat," the hint[4] might be the word "frog." This maintains sufficient security as long as the frequency measures of the *remaining* words are sufficiently low.

Our new structure allows for a class of new features that are not supported by the traditional password paradigm – such as voice-based entry and the use of equivalence classes. Equivalence classes – such as normalizing different tenses of verbs – permit the adaptation of the authentication mechanism to how people remember and enter credentials. This includes order invariance where "flat frog work' would be considered equivalent to "frog work flat." It also includes synonyms (making "fat cat bite" equivalent to "chubby kitty chomp"), and homophones and their approximations (making "red flower fly" equivalent to "read flour fry"). The latter helps with voice entry of credentials.

Yet another benefit of our proposed technique is that it allows for a crude determination (on the backend) of the *degree* of correctness of a given login attempt, in contrast to what can be done in traditional password systems. While this type of data should never be fed back to the user (or it can be used as an oracle to attack the system), it can aid in the collection of analytics on the backend. The fuzziness is achieved at the cost of a slight expansion of the records used to store salted and hashed credentials, but without any associated reduction of security.

Outline: We begin by describing related work in section 6.2. We detail the basic structure of our proposal in section 4.3 – both from the point of view of the user experience and in terms of the backend solution. We then describe how to achieve an extended feature set in section 4.4. Examples of such extended features include voice-entry of fastwords and hints given to users who fail to log in. We report on a usability study in section 6.5, wherein we compare recall rates for different types of credentials. We then describe our adversarial model and provide security analysis of our proposal in section 4.6. In section 4.7, we report on a second usability experiment that lets us establish speed of entry for passwords and fastwords on handsets and traditional keyboards.

---

[4] Some fastwords would have one word hints. This could be the first or the least common word, for example.

4.2 Related Work

Typical typists enter on average 33 words per minute on a regular keyboard, according to a study by Karat et al. [55]. MacKenzie and Soukoreff [62] estimate that the
mean entry rate is typically in the range of 15 to 30 words per minute for on-screen
keyboards without error correction, while Kristensson and Zhai [57] show that it
is common for users to reach 45 words per minute on on-screen keyboards if error
correction *is* used. It is clear that the entry rates go down for any of these cases if
the user has to make extra key presses to change case or to shift between letters,
numerals and "special" characters, but we are not aware of any previous study that
measures this effect. On an iPhone each capitalization costs one extra click, as does
each shift to/from numerals and special characters. This means, for example, that
"flY2theM0On!," *requires* 21 clicks, in spite of having only twelve characters. We
performed timing experiments on various platforms and found that the amount of
time taken to type simple credentials like fastwords almost doubles when using a
mobile device instead of a traditional keyboard.

The handset market is increasingly moving towards soft buttons, as opposed to
hardware keyboards as is standard for traditional computers. This leads to a higher
rate of errors. Lee and Zhai [60] report that when data is entered using fingers (as
opposed to a stylus), then the error rate is 8% higher for soft buttons than for hard
buttons. (This result is from a study without tactile or audio feedback, where the
sizes of the soft and hard buttons were approximately the same.)

Traditional password strength checking is a heuristic approach that provides
some estimates on the strength of the credential. Different service providers implement vastly different approaches, which explains why one password may be considered strong by one provider and weak by another. Our proposed credential strength
checker will still rely on heuristics, but with an underpinning of quantifiable metrics,
such as the frequencies of single words, word pairs, and more generally, any n-tuple
of words. This is referred to as an N-gram. In this study, we use Microsoft's Web N-
Gram Service [93]. However, the word frequencies can be relative to any preferred
source, such as standard spoken English, tweets, or already registered credentials –
although the latter must be determined in a way that does not compromise the in-
tegrity of individual credentials. Therefore, while our proposed strength checker is
not perfect, it *is* based on more clearly enunciated metrics than password strength
checkers, given that our proposed credentials have a simpler structure than good
passwords do.

It is known that the more concrete and meaningful information is, the easier it
is to remember [25]. We use sequences of dictionary words to enable easy error
correction and simplify recall. We measure both the speed of entering credentials
and their recall, relative to other common types of credentials.

The use of dictionary words as credentials is not new. This approach was used
both by Compuserve and AOL in the mid-eighties. As a user would sign up, she
would be assigned a password that consisted of two dictionary words with some
connector. Compuserve, for example, used the format expressed by the sample pass-

word "evening_crucial." Neither Compuserve's nor AOL's scheme can take advantage of error-correction techniques, nor were they designed to do so.

S/KEY, a one-time password system for Unix systems, translates 64-bit one-time passwords to sequences of words by mapping the bit strings to six words drawn from a public 2048-word dictionary. The use of words in S/KEY was to improve usability of entering keys, and not to take advantage of error-correction or mnemonics.

Similarly, Bard [5] and Cheswick [14] independently proposed a technique in which users are assigned a collection of words as their credential. In those schemes, the collection of words is drawn uniformly at random from a large set of words that exhibit optimal distance characteristics from other selectable words. This permits error correction of words within this dictionary. The Bard approach emphasizes maximum error correction, resulting in system-selected credentials potentially containing words like "abarticular" and "galaxidae,"[5] which is likely to cause user consternation. In contrast, our goals are pragmatic: to maximize authentication success and speed. We achieve this by allowing the user to select her own credential. While our error correction does not have theoretically optimal properties, it is practical, and our system can use *standard* auto-correction and -completion algorithms.[6]

Turning to the security of a credential, it is worth noting that there are two appropriate but very distinct security measures worth considering. One aims at assessing the complexity of passwords, then equating security with complexity. (This is what traditional password strength checkers do.) The other focuses solely on avoiding the weakest (i.e., most common) credentials, since these are what most attackers try. In a sense, traditional password strength checkers do this using a manually entered list of passwords that are believed to be weak. Another more elegant approach was proposed by Schechter et al. [81]. Their technique automatically avoids common passwords without any explicit identification of what these are. Our structure supports both of these approaches. The *observed* commonality of a fastword can be determined using methods analogous to those described in [81]; moreover, the *estimated* likelihood can be computed using the frequencies of words and their combinations – to produce a more fine-grained strength estimate than is possible for passwords. The ability to break down a credential into its components and determine the likelihood of the combination makes it possible to detect and avoid common phrases – whether by relying on search engines, a corpus of common phrases, or simply N-gram services. This makes it possible to avoid weak credentials, which otherwise is a security risk associated with mnemonic passwords [59].

We describe voice-based entry of fastwords. Voice-based authentication was studied by Monrose et al. [65]; however, they focused on *how* a phrase was spoken – not just what the phrase was. The voice-based entry in our proposal is not

---

[5] These are actual examples from [5]. However, while words known only by linguists could surely be filtered out, it is indisputable that user-selected credentials have better recall rates than schemes based on assigned credentials.

[6] On a handset, this is trivial: We simply do not disable the auto-correction/completion features, as is done for traditional passwords. It is also possible to have auto-correction/completion on traditional computers, where it can be added either as a client-side plugin, a JavaScript snippet, or a server-side feature.

about biometrics, but simply a matter of what user interface we rely on for the entry of the fastword. As a result, we can use standard dictation tools to interpret and perform error correction of the audio data. Using equivalence classes, we can avoid problems associated with lack of precision without having to train the system on the level of individuals.

4.3 Your Credential is A Story

User experience. The user experience of entering fastwords will be very similar to that of entering passwords – except with the added benefits endowed by error-correction and auto-completion features. Instead of entering a password, the user would simply enter a sequence of words, separated by spaces. As a user completes a word, the word can be shown for an instant before each letter of the word is replaced by a star. As with traditional passwords, the user would press enter at the end of the sequence. This user experience is the same when fastwords are *registered* (enrollment) and when they are *used* (authentication.) A credential strength meter can be used to indicate the quality of what has been entered during enrollment. A sample user interface is shown in figure 4.1.

Fig. 4.1 What the user may see when entering a fastword. The first word has been replaced by stars and the second word is shown with an auto-correct suggestion. The use of auto-correct and auto-complete allows users to type faster and with less precision. To accept a suggestion, the user simply presses SPACE and continues writing the next word – or presses ENTER or SUBMIT to conclude. To turn down a suggestion – which should typically not happen in the context of fastword entry – the user taps the X next to the suggestion.

Client-side process. In contrast to text entry, traditional password entry does not rely on error-correction techniques. The incorrect password submission simply triggers the event which asks the user to try again. Fastword entry is instead implemented like regular text entry, which means that auto-correction and auto-completion are not *disabled*, and therefore, *automatically* performed in the selected language.

Analogous to how characters are often replaced by stars or other characters during password entry (whether immediately or as the next character is entered), completed words can be replaced by stars during fastword entry. This can be achieved using JavaScript or an embedded program such as Flash or Java applet.

The credential is transmitted over an encrypted channel to a backend server in charge of enrollment or authentication; this can be done in installments (e.g., after each keyword) or after the entire fastword has been entered. The backend server then signals back whether the credential is accepted or not. For enrollment, this corresponds to communicating the result of a credential strength check (described below). For authentication it is simply a matter of signaling success or failure.

Backend process.

- **Credential strength checker.** As a new credential is submitted, whether as an account is set up or to replace another credential, the credential strength checker is used to verify that the credential is sufficiently strong.

  The credential strength checker determines the product of single-word frequencies of the words in a credential, and uses that as one strength estimate. The strength checker also determines the N-gram frequency of the sequence, and uses that as a second estimate. These two security assessments are performed relative to frequencies in the English language (e.g., using the Microsoft Web N-Gram Service [93]) and relative to already registered fastwords. If any of these measures indicates that the new credential is more likely than a system security threshold (such as 2^{-30}) then the credential is rejected.

  The output of the credential strength checker is the inverse of the highest result from the other checkers, which is the estimated probability with which the adversary is expected to be able to guess the credential. Alternatively, it can be represented as the minimum of the bits of security of the two tests, i.e., the negative second logarithm of the associated frequency.

- **Dictionary words.** In contrast to typical passwords, it is not desirable for the user to include non-dictionary words in a fastword. This is because the auto-completion feature on the client device would *learn* these new terms eventually – which inevitably means *storing* them. This is undesirable from a security stance. To avoid this, the server-side will verify that all words are dictionary words when the user registers a fastword. (It would either have to ask the user what language is used, or infer it from the words used.)

- **Enrollment.** After a credential has been determined to be strong, it is accepted and then stored on the backend. Just as passwords are salted and hashed to reduce the risk of internal exposure, so are fastwords. More specifically, if the credential is a k-tuple of words, $W = (w_1, w_2, \ldots, w_k)$, then $hash(W, salt)$ is stored along with the unique value $salt$.

- **Normalization of credentials.** We assume the use of some amount of normalization, whether for robustness or to add system features. An example of the former type of normalization is for all credentials to be converted to lower-case representations before they are salted and hashed. As an example of a feature-extending type of normalization, one may sort the words of the fastwords in order to obtain order invariance.

- **Conventional authentication.** The server looks up the appropriate user record (given the username or other identifier), and salts and hashes the normalized credential to be verified, comparing the result with the stored result. More specifically, the value *salt* is extracted from the database, $hash(W, salt)$ is computed, where W is the normalized credential to be verified. If the result of the hash matches the stored result, the authentication is said to have succeeded.

- **Application.** The technique we describe can be used both to authenticate from handsets to remote sites, and to the handsets themselves. In the latter case, an external service could be involved during the fastword registration phase in order to verify the strength of the credential – it is not practically feasible to house this database on a handset. If no strength check is needed, this outsourcing is also not required.

We report on relative recall rates for different types of credentials in section refrec; analyze the security of our construction in section 4.6; and the speed on credential entry in section 4.7. In the next section, we describe an extended feature set based on the techniques we have just described.

4.4 Extended Feature Set

There is an array of new features that are made possible by the new structure we use – and, in particular, by the decomposability of the credential. We will now describe some of these features.

Use of conceptual equivalence classes. One can use conceptual equivalence classes to allow for *variants* of a word to be accepted, which aims at establishing the intent of the user when she enters a credential. The use of conceptual equivalence classes[7] addresses a situation in which some words are largely interchangeable to users, a situation which could otherwise potentially create difficulties if a user has to remember the exact word she used. As a simple example, an equivalence class may contain different tenses of a given verb – for example, to avoid a distinction to be made between the word "run" and the word "running." Equivalence classes may also be used to allow substitution of words of similar meaning. For example, a user entering a fastword (mother, stroke, wedding) during enrollment may later attempt to authenticate using the sequence (mom, stroke, wedding) or (mother, rub, wedding) – depending on whether the person uses multiple terms to refer to his/her mother, and based on the intended meaning of "stroke". (There is no attempt to infer the meaning of a word on the backend in the current proof-of-concept implementation.)

Given a credential $W = (w_1, w_2, \ldots, w_k)$ as input, the backend computes $E(W) = E(w_1), E(w_2), \ldots, E(w_k))$, where E is the function that maps a word to its equivalence class. Instead of computing $hash(W, salt)$ for a given value *salt*, the backend would compute $hash(E(W), salt)$ – whether for the purposes of enrollment or authentication.

---

[7] It is straightforward to generate some conceptual equivalence relations, e.g., for tenses and synonyms, but not clear how to generate a complete collection.

Use of homophonic equivalence classes. One can use a normalization corresponding to homophonic equivalence classes to simplify voice-based[8] entry of credentials. We assume the use of standard dictation tools to create a mapping from the audio sample to a homophonic equivalence class; this corresponds to the error-correction processing of text inputs. To avoid having to train the tool on individual speakers (as dictation tools need), we will combine this with wide equivalence classes. This will map a large number of words, along with different pronunciations and accents, to the same equivalence class.[9] The resulting equivalence classes are phonetic representations of the words of the fastword. To process the credential, the backend would salt and hash the sequence of phonetic representations to create the credential record.

The creation of homophonic equivalence classes, and the associated credential records could be done *in addition* to the other credential records created and maintained on the backend. During voice-based authentication, the candidate credential would be verified by being represented by its phonetic description, salted, hashed, and compared to the stored record.

Implementing fuzzy authentication. Instead of storing a salted hash of the *full* credential W during the enrollment process, the backend server stores salted hashes of all acceptable variants, using the same salt for each such variant. This is done in a manner that does not reveal the number of words k of the credential, where $k \leq k_{max}$. If we set $k_{max} = 4$ words, then there are no more than four subsets of the credential, in which one word has been omitted, and one verbatim credential. If a credential has fewer than k_{max} words, then the remaining slots in the record would store random strings of the correct format. This way, one cannot infer the value k from a user record on the backend.

To perform *fuzzy* verification of a submitted credential during an attempted login, it is checked against each of the stored credentials by salting and hashing it, comparing the result to the stored values. One can also verify that it has no more than k_{max} words, and test all subsets of size $k_{max} - 1$ to see if either matches the stored values.

If the submitted credential, after being salted and hashed, matches the stored full credentials then the login attempt is successful. If either of the comparisons with the subset credentials results in equality, then the submitted credential is known to be *almost* correct. It is a matter of policy to react to *almost* correct credentials. The backend server may consider it a successful login attempt or permit limited access, or other system actions may be taken. Users are not given any feedback describing the degree to which their credential was correct, or this could be used as a password breaking oracle.

Implementing hints. If a user forgets her fastword, she can be given a hint, which is one of the words in her fastword. It would always be the same word for a partic-

---

[8] The issue of eavesdropping is an orthogonal problem to the management of audio authentication, and is not addressed in this chapter.

[9] One might argue that it is enough that the sequence sounds *the same* during registration and authentication; however, the use of wide equivalence classes permits text-based registration followed by voice-based authentication.

ular user and fastword; it could be either the first word or the word with the lowest frequency – this is fairly likely to provide the most help to the user. The hint is also selected so that the frequency measures of the *remaining* words in the fastword correspond to a sufficiently secure credential.[10] In section 6.5, we report on the extent to which hints help users recall a credential, based on a user study we performed.

Implementing fuzzy blacklists. If a given user's credentials are believed or known to have been compromised (e.g., by a phisher or malware), then the exposed credential can be placed on a user-specific blacklist. This would block the user from using this credential – or one with a large overlap – later on. This is to address the problem that users have "credential classes" and there is a large degree of reuse – even after a credential has been corrupted!

4.5 Recall Rates

We performed an experiment in which we recruited users to set up a collection of different credentials, and attempt to authenticate between 2-3 weeks later. (On average, the authentication took place 20 days after the setup.) To incentivize participation, we raffled off an iPad2 among all subjects that completed the study, independently of "performance". A total of 147 subjects enrolled in the study; 105 completed it.

The aim of the study was to determine what types of credentials are easiest to recall, relative to each other. For this reason, we asked subjects not to reuse credentials from elsewhere, as this would bias their ability to recall these, and provide the authors with valid real-life credentials for these subjects, which we did not want to obtain. Furthermore, we asked the subjects to promise that they would not write down any credentials.

We asked subjects to create five types of credentials: a "simple password" (such as what they might use for a social networking service); a "strong password" (such as what they may use for financial transactions; a 4-digit PIN; a 6-digit PIN; and a three-word fastword. We also asked them to remember a "super-strong password" – a complex password we assigned to them. For each credential, we asked them to assess how likely they would be to remember it after 2-3 weeks. In the second phase of the experiment, we asked them to recall the credentials and state whether they believe they managed to do so.

Subjects were considered to have succeeded with an authentication if they managed to enter the credential verbatim during the authentication stage – except for the fastwords where capitalization, tense, and order were not considered, and subjects who entered at least two of the three words were passed. This matches the way real authentication would be performed. Subjects who failed the fastword authentication

---

[10] We note that if a hint has *ever* been given for a given fastword without a successful authentication following in the same session, then the word that corresponds to the hint should be considered public. This must be considered in the context of fuzzy verification.

were given a hint – the first word of their fastword – and asked to try again. Subjects who failed the strong password authentication were given a second chance too, but no hint. This also matches the way real authentication would be performed.

Table 4.1 Recall rates for various types of credentials

| | Recall rates | |
Credential	User estimate	Measured
Simple passwords	24%	14%
Strong passwords	22%	6%
– addl. after reminder	10%	0%
Super-strong passwords	5%	2%
4-digit PIN	47%	26%
6-digit PIN	28%	29%
3-word fastword	25%	36%
– addl. after hint	65%	48%

The recall rates of the various credentials are shown in table 4.1. The subjects guess whether they correctly recalled a credential done on a 5-point Likert scale, where we count the responses "I think I did," "very likely," and "certain" as a vote of confidence, while "maybe" and "I did not" were counted as a lack of confidence. We see that people remember passwords to a lesser extent than they expect, and fastwords to a greater extent. The lower success rates for the 4-digit PINs in comparison to the 4-digit PINs (in spite of the subject's expectations) could be explained by the fact that a greater number of subjects reused[11] their 4-digit PINs than their 6-digit PINs – probably since 4-digit PINs are more common than 6-digit PINs – and then failed to remember *which* PIN they used.

While this does not show how well people would recall any of these credentials in a real-life scenario, it shows how well they remember them relative to each other, in a setting where they are not strongly incentivized to do well. The experiment shows that users are able to recall fastwords to a much greater extent than passwords, and that close to half of those who forget their fastwords are helped by the hint given. For actual success rates, it may be necessary to perform a more realistic experiment in which users are better incentivized to recall their credentials.

As part of the study, we collected some demographic information. Among other things, we asked subjects to indicate their profession. We could not identify any relation between profession and performance, and in particular, did not see different recall rates among technical people, who were overrepresented in the study in relation to their relative number in society.

---

[11] In spite of being instructed not to reuse credentials, 20% of the subjects admitted to reusing a 4-digit PIN, in contrast to only 10% for 6-digit PINs.

4.6 Security Analysis

We want to compare the strength of the fastword with that of traditional passwords. We will begin by reviewing the approximate security of passwords (section 4.6), followed by an adversarial model for our context (section 4.6), and an analysis of the security of fastwords (section 4.6).

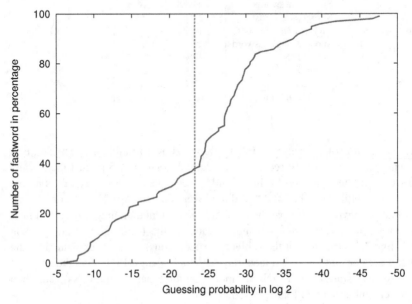

Fig. 4.2 The figure shows a cumulative distribution of the conditional probabilities of fastwords in our user study after the word with the *lowest frequency* has been given as a hint. After the hint is given, 61% of the fastwords have a security that exceeds the average security of passwords.

The Security of Passwords

NIST [13] estimates that the average distribution of passwords corresponds to an entropy of 4 bits for the first character, 2 bits for the next seven characters, 1.5 bits per character for the ninth to the 20th character, and 1 bit per character for the remainder of the password. 6 bits of entropy is added when the user is forced to use both uppercase and non-alphabetic characters. This is for traditional passwords – mobile passwords are likely to have lower entropy due to the complications of entering them – at least in contexts where the user is aware of later having to enter the password on a mobile platform when first selecting it. There are also indications that users select passwords of varying strength for different types of sites. Analysis [44] of passwords from raided dropboxes suggests that the average password length was 7.9 characters, which corresponds to an entropy of approximately 18 bits. While this indicates that the *average* probability of guessing a password is 2^{-18}, an attacker can gain access to a fairly large portion of accounts simply by trying the most common credentials – this probability is on the order of $0.22 - 0.9\%$ [85, 39].

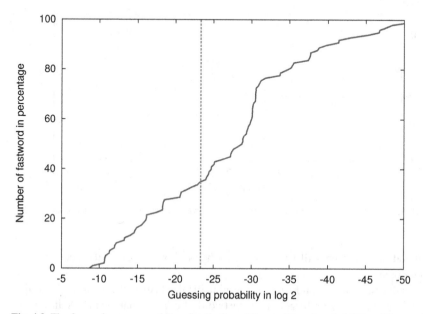

Fig. 4.3 The figure shows a cumulative distribution of the conditional probabilities of fastwords in our user study after the *first* keyword of the fastword has been given as a hint. 64% of the fastwords have a security that exceeds the average security of passwords after the hint is given.

Understanding the Adversary

We consider a remote adversary attempting to gain illegitimate access to an account. We assume that the adversary knows the rules used to approve and reject fastwords as they are first established, and that he knows system-wide weights and parameters. We also assume that he knows the frequencies of individual words and N-grams. We make the pessimistic assumption that the system does *not* know the true frequencies, but that it misestimates them by factor c.

The adversary wishes to guess the fastword of a given user. Since we may assume that an adversary will behave rationally, we know that he will try the most likely fastword candidates (that would be accepted by the system) in order of decreasing

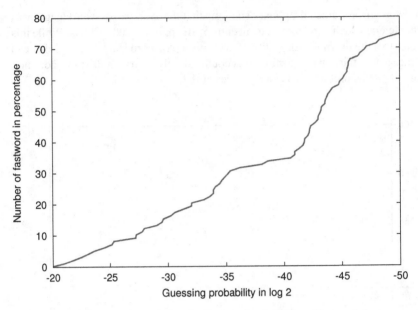

Fig. 4.4 The figure shows a cumulative distribution of probabilities of fastwords in our user study.

likelihood, and that he will try as many as he is allowed before the account gets locked down.

The adversary will request to get the hint for the fastword (claiming to be the targeted user t and having forgotten the fastword.) Let's say that the hint is displayed to the adversary – as opposed to being sent to an email address associated with the account. The adversary then attempts to guess the two missing words in a manner that maximizes his probability of success. We say that the adversary *wins* if he manages to get access to the targeted account.

Note that we do not focus on security against shoulder surfing or eavesdropping, nor attacks in which the adversary knows his victim.[12] These are interesting attacks to consider, but are not the primary threats in most systems, and are beyond the scope of this chapter.

The Security of Fastwords

We have assumed an adversary who knows the true frequencies and distributions of words and fastwords, obtains the hint for a given fastword, and who then attempts to guess the remaining two words. Let us also assume that a person will be given n chances to log in to an account from an unknown IP address.

---

[12] It is worth noting that most systems are rather vulnerable against adversaries who know the victim, due to the poor security of many password reset schemes [80].

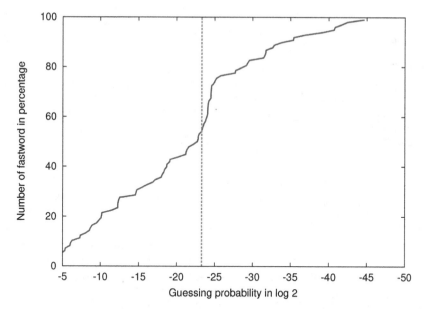

Fig. 4.5 The figure shows a cumulative distribution of the conditional probabilities of fastwords in our user study with equivalence classes of size $s = 8$ added. This assumes that the adversary has obtained the *first* keyword of the fastword after this is given as a hint. 45% of the fastwords have a security that exceeds the average security of passwords. We note that fastwords with lower security can be rejected at enrollment. Alternatively, hints can be disabled for these credentials, or smaller sets of equivalence classes be used.

We will let $\hat{f}$ denote an upper bound of the the actual frequencies of the n most likely fastwords conditional on the hint. This corresponds to a probability of success for the adversary of no more than $p = 1 - (1 - \hat{f})^n$. This is the same as stating that $\hat{f} = 1 - (1-p)^{1/n}$. Since we have assumed that the system's understanding of frequencies would be off by factor c, this corresponds to requiring that the system's belief of the conditional frequency of a fastword, given the hint, is $f \leq (1 - (1-p)^{1/n})/c$.

For concreteness, we may set the maximum probability of success for the attacker to $p = 2^{-20}$. Recalling the analysis in section 4.6, this corresponds to a *minimum* security of the solution exceeding the *average* security of typical passwords by 2 bits. We further assume $n = 5$ and $c = 2$. Given the hint, these parameter choices corresponds to a conditional frequency of the fastword no greater than $2^{-23.3}$.

In figure 4.2, we show the conditional probabilities of fastwords used by subjects in our study, given the word with the lowest frequency as a hint. In figure 4.3, we instead plot the conditional probability based on using the first keyword in the fastword as a hint. In both graphs, we draw a line at the probability of $2^{-23.3}$, as described above. We see that 61% vs. 64% of the fastwords have conditional probabilities (for the adversary to succeed) that correspond to a fastword security that is better than the *average* password security and *much* better than the *lowest* password

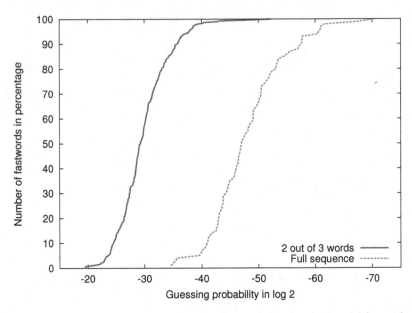

Fig. 4.6 The figure shows the cumulative distribution of the strength of partial fastwords of one hundred subjects where two out of the three keywords are entered and the third left out. We show all combinations; thus, the above corresponds to the average security. For comparison, we also show the strength of complete fastwords for the same set of subjects. Recall that typical passwords are believed to have 18 bits [13] of security.

security. If this is the minimum acceptable security, then fastwords that do not comply can either be rejected during the enrollment phase, or the system may refuse to disclose hints for these values.

In figure 4.4, we show the cumulative distribution of fastwords in our study where hints are *not* given or interceptable by a typical attacker. All of these measures use the minimum-security estimate after computing the N-gram frequency and the product of frequencies.

We have not discussed the security against an adversary who gains access to the salted and hashed fastwords, and to the hints, which must be stored in cleartext on the backend. However, this can easily be seen to correspond to the security shown in figures 4.2 and 4.3. We note that if the system policy is to never give out a hint if the resulting security would fall below a system threshold, then these hints do not need to be stored.

Turning now to the security of the extended feature set, we observe that this depends on the number and sizes of the equivalence classes. For simplicity, we assume that *all* words belong to equivalence classes, and that each class contains exactly s elements. The probability of being able to guess the sequence will be increased by a factor of s^n where n is a number of words in a sequence. For $n = 3$ words in a fastword, as we have used, and for equivalence classes of size $s = 8$ words, this means

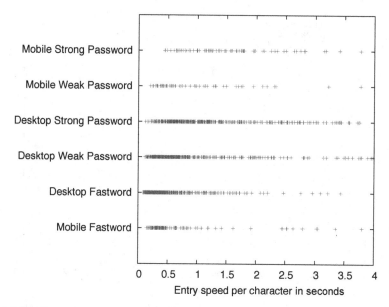

Fig. 4.7 The figure shows a scatter plot of how long participants in the study took to enter passwords and fastwords on handsets and traditional keyboards. Note that we did not implement error correction for the desktop fastwords in this study; this could easily be done in a real-world application using a scripting language.

a reduction of security by a factor 2^9 for the entire fastword and 2^6 for the fastword given a hint.

In other words, a fastword whose probability of being guessed is 2^{-42} would be guessable with a probability of 2^{-33} if equivalence classes are used, and these each have the maximum size of $s = 8$. Similarly, if the probability of success for an adversary would be 2^{-27} after seeing the hint, then the use of equivalence classes of size $s = 8$ would increase this to a probability of success of 2^{-21}.

In figure 4.5, we show the effects on security of using such equivalence classes. The graph describes the conditional fastword probabilities, given the first keyword as a hint.

We note that a realistic implementation will have differing sizes of equivalence classes. While we use a somewhat simplified analysis by assuming that all equivalence classes are of the same size, this does not affect the underlying principles. Moreover, we note that the sizes of equivalence classes can be set to balance usability needs and security expectations.

Similarly, if the system accepts a login attempt with only a partial match to the registered fastword, this affects security. It is possible to set a threshold for the minimum security required. For example, if *one* subset of keywords correspond to a sufficiently low frequency measure, while *another* does not, then the first would be accepted but the second would not. (At least not without any additional support for the login attempt.) It is also possible that an authentication above one level gives ac-

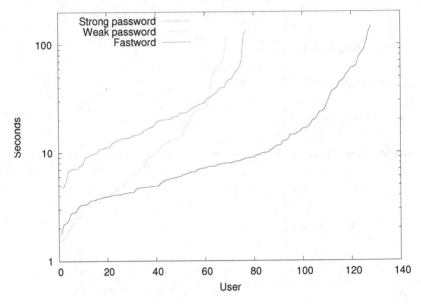

Fig. 4.8 This plot shows the time taken to enter each type of credential (strong password, weak password, and fastword) by different users. The plot is sorted in ascending order. It should be noted that points with the same "User" number do not come from the same user. Fastwords are quicker to enter for most users; however, they could be slower for users who do not use their phone to type; these users "peck out" any credential, and the entry time depends to a large extent on the length of the credential.

cess to certain resources, whereas an authentication above another level gives access to others. To illustrate the effect of partial matches on security, we plot the security resulting from inputting only two out of the three keywords for the fastwords of our one hundred subjects. In figure 4.6, we show all combinations of keyword selections herein – in other words, a total of 300 partial matches for our 100 subjects.

4.7 Entry Speed

In addition to being able to assess the security and recall rates of fastwords relative to traditional passwords, we *also* wish to estimate how long it takes to enter these types of credentials on a typical handset.

This was done in a second user study. We recruited participants to enter three fastwords and three passwords on a device where the credentials used were drawn at random from the credentials obtained from the study described in section 6.5. Half of the passwords were what we refer to as "simple" passwords and the other half, "strong." These correspond to passwords the participants in the first study gave as example passwords for social networking sites and financial sites, respectively.

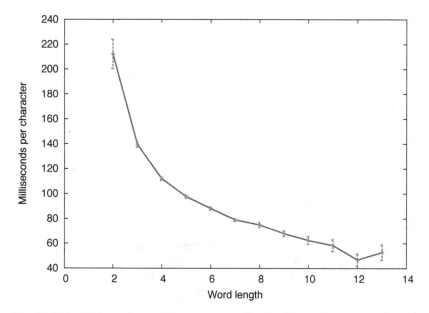

Fig. 4.9 This plot shows the speed in average time taken in milliseconds to enter each character of a word. The plot shows that the longer the word, the shorter the average time it takes to enter each character. Confidence intervals are marked.

Subjects were told to enter the credentials as fast as they could then shown the time taken to enter them.

We recruited a total of 234 PC users and 45 mobile users from Amazon Mechanical Turk, friends and family, and tweets. The browser agent was read to determine what type of device each subject used. The timing results are shown in figures 4.7 and 4.8. While error correction can be added to desktop text entry using plugins or backend correction, this was not done herein, and therefore, timing for fastwords on desktops are upper estimates.

We note that the subjects entered unknown credentials – therefore, there is no speedup due to "motoric memory" of having repeatedly entered the same string. That effect has to be determined through follow-up studies. However, we note that it is reasonable to expect that motoric memory will affect both fastwords and passwords – the extent to which it will reduce the entry time is likely to depend largely on the length of the credential.

It is shown in the experiment that fastwords can be entered faster than normal passwords, but the number of participants and the variety of fastwords were too few to make the result conclusive. Therefore, to understand the effect on the speed of entering the credentials, we conducted another longer term experiment to measure fastword entering speed. The experiment required participants to enter a random three-word fastword daily for 20 days. In order to limit the effect of the platform on the word-suggestion and auto-correction, we limited the mobile devices to Android-

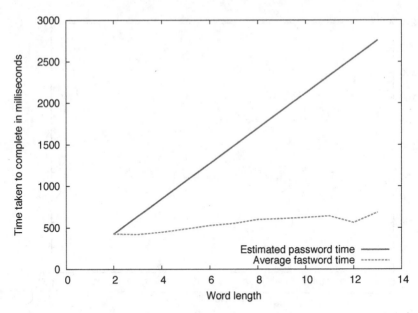

Fig. 4.10 This plot shows the average time taken in milliseconds to enter a word. The plot also shows an estimated time to enter a password with the same length. Neither of these take motorc memory into consideration, but it is expected that this would affect both credential types in the same manner.

based devices. The result from 409 participants is shown in figure 4.9. The plot shows that fastwords can take advantage of word-suggestion and auto-correction to allow a much faster entry of a credential than a typical password system. As shown in figure 4.10, the length of words in a fastword do not significantly increase the input time compared to entering a password with the same length. This finding implies that a user can increase the number of words in a fastword to five words and spend as much time to enter them as it would take to enter a 14-character password. However, a secure five-word fastword can be much easier to remember than a secure 14-character password.

Chapter 5
Improved Visual Preference Authentication

Markus Jakobsson, Hossein Siadati

Abstract

We describe a preference-based authentication scheme in which both security and usability of previous approaches are dramatically improved upon. We report on experimental findings supporting a false negative rate on the order[1] of 0.9% and a false positive rate on the order of 0.5% for a choice of parameters that result in a registration time of 100 seconds and an authentication time of 40 seconds.

5.1 Preference-Based Authentication

Passwords are a fact of modern life, but so is *forgetting* them [3]. Security questions are widely used as a self-serve approach to resetting passwords, to avoid the substantial costs of involving a customer representative [92]. However, it is well understood that security questions are weak [33, 51, 53, 73, 84, 86, 102].

At the same time, as attackers can often guess or infer the answers to security questions, many users also fail to answer *their own* challenge questions. This is sometimes believed to be due to inconsistent spelling ("Garden Street" becomes "Garden St."); forgotten *false* answers ("What is your mother's middle name?" "Abraham Lincoln."); and even forgotten *true* answers. The latter is made more common by an increased reliance on obscure questions [74].

To make matters worse, the same questions are extensively used by different service providers, causing users to rely on the same *answers* to authenticate in many places. Like the use of the same password on many sites, this is a security liability.

At the heart of the problem of backup authentication are two main issues at odds with each other. On one hand, the user has to be able to successfully authenticate – even if this is an infrequent action. This suggests the need to avoid authentication using obscure facts. On the other hand, in order to thwart impostors with data-mining skills or personal knowledge of the victims, "obvious" facts need to be avoided.. It was long believed that letting the user write her own security questions would help address these problems, but that was shown to be absolutely wrong by Just et al. [54]: Users produce questions with low entropy answers, and are not as good as expected in remembering answers to their own questions.

---

[1] For precise estimates of error rates, large-scale testing is necessary.

M. Jakobsson, *Mobile Authentication*, SpringerBriefs in Computer Science, DOI: 10.1007/978-1-4614-4878-5_5, © The Author(s) 2013

Preference-based authentication [48, 50] strikes a reasonable balance between these two conflicting requirements, as preferences are more stable than long-term memory, but a large class of preferences (namely those that are not very strong) are not commonly made public. Existing methods share one practical problem, though: it takes too long for a user to register. For example, to attain a false positive rate below 1% and a false negative rate of 2.5%, a system user described in [68] has to select 12 things he likes and 12 things he dislikes from a list of choices, and later select at least 10 of his likes from the 24 images. Registration is reported to take almost 170 seconds and authentication just below 60 seconds. In contrast, we obtain lower similar error rates with a registration process that takes only 100 seconds, and an authentication process taking 40 seconds.

The time improvement for registration and authentication is due to several novel techniques. First of all, the authentication process is a tertiary classification (*like*, *dislike*, and *no opinion*) instead of a binary classification (*likes* and *dislikes*). Since this gives rise to a larger number of combinations, one can obtain the same level of security with a smaller number of selections. To compensate for the fact that users will make what we call "small mistakes" – the classification of a *no opinion* image as a *like* or *dislike*, or vice versa – one can have a more generous threshold for this type of mistake than for what we call "big mistakes" – the classification of a *like* as a *dislike*, or vice versa.

Second, the user is asked to identify her likes and dislikes only during the registration and authentication phases, and the no opinion selections are inferred from user choices. For a typical user, more than 80% of the available choices belong to the no opinion category, which is what makes this approach a big efficiency improvement. We describe a simple but effective trick to make sure that the system does not incorrectly identify items as belonging to the no opinion category during the registration phase– this could otherwise cause false negatives during the authentication phase.

Using these techniques, the user only needs to identify three likes and dislikes each during the registration phase – then, during the authentication phase, identify the three things he likes and three things he dislikes from a collection of 12 images. Since the system deduced that the user had no strong opinion of the 6 "extra" images, this classification results in a very low risk for errors. (We describe several other parameter choices as well and compare the resulting error rates with each other.)

Outline

We review related work (section 5.2), describe features of the novel approach (section 5.3), then detail the solution (section 5.4). After that, we describe our experimental setup (section 5.5) and analyze the associated results (section 5.6).

5.2 Related Work

Human-to-computer authentication systems – excluding biometric systems – are typically vulnerable to automated credential guessing attacks and attacks by people close to the victim. Examples of automated attacks on PINs and passwords were described by Bonneau et al [12] and Bonneau [9], respectively. Common challenge questions were addressed by Rabkin [74]. Schechter et al. [79] demonstrated the ease with which people can guess the answers to challenge questions of their acquaintances, friends and family members.

Password reset is the last resort of users who have forgotten and are unable to recall or recover their credentials. It is well understood that when it comes to security, password reset is commonly the weakest link [10, 15, 73]: There is only a small number of so-called challenge questions that are meaningful, which means that many sites use the same questions and many users rely on the same credentials to access different accounts. Even so, the questions used by major service providers posed difficulties to half of the users: 20% of whom forgot the answers within six months; 17Since using only one security question poses a risk, especially for traditional security questions, a combination of authentication methods to verify user identity has been suggested [82].

While Yan et al. [101] conclude that memorability and security are not at odds with each other by *necessity*, it is clear that, for many authentication instances, they *are*. It has been argued [48] that the principal weakness of security questions are that they rely on *facts*. These facts have to be *remembered* by users, and should not be easy for attackers to *learn*. Shifting from a fact-based approach to a preference-based approach improves the permanence of the challenge, since preferences are more stable than long-term memory. At the same time, avoiding topics that arouse very strong opinions (such as specific sports teams) makes it less likely that a user will accidentally disclose the answers – whether to people in their surroundings or on social networks. This is done by asking users to classify concepts based on their associated preferences – whether they like or dislike the concepts; the system then determines whether a user is legitimate or not by comparing the answers to previously recorded preferences.

Visual preference authentication uses techniques set forth in the previously cited work on preference-based authentication [48, 50], replacing textual descriptions of concepts with images. The change to a visual interface decreased registration and authentication times, and improved user experience. However, by relying on a binary classification during authentication, all these approaches require a relatively large number of selections for security reasons. The current work improves on this by going beyond a binary classification with two classes; *likes* and *dislikes*. It may seem at first that one can derive even greater system security by expanding the sets of such classes – for example, to correspond to things the user *loves*, *likes*, has *no opinion* about, *dislikes*, and *hates*. However, early experiments [48] suggest that while diametric changes of preference (e.g., *likes* becoming *dislikes*) are extremely rare, and partial shifts of preference (e.g., *no opinions* becoming *likes*), rare, it is very common for degrees of *likes* and *dislikes* to get mixed up. For example, a user may state initially that she *likes* pizza, only to say that she *loves* it when prompted closer to lunchtime. We describe a practical way to obtain tertiary classification while reducing user effort, using an automated infernal of items in the newly added class.

Orthogonal to the issues of false negatives and security against a typical online attacker, Hayashi et al. [34] studied how to harden an image-based authentication system against an attack by a person close to the victim, such as a family member. They found that partial obfuscation of images helped. Similarly, labeling images in addition to image obfuscation was studied to resolve the same issue[22].

Other types of graphical authentication methods have also been proposed and studied [70, 21, 95]; those approaches are not based on preferences but recall. Similarly, authentication methods based on recall of activities and events have been proposed [4]. Another approach is to employ social authentication, in which a user's contacts help her gain access to her account [83]. Yet other approaches bootstrap authentication on access to a device used to store a secret [63], or relying on associative memory [75].

5.3 Approach

It is helpful to consider the proposed solution in the context of previous preference-based authentication methods. The principles of these are illustrated in figure 5.1. We consider two phases: registration and authentication. In the registration phase, the user identifies a number of *likes* and *dislikes* from a large pool of candidates. During the authentication phase, he is asked to identify which of the previous selections he likes. The system determines whether it is the proper user based on the number of correct identifications the user makes. Although this approach works well, it requires a fairly large number of selections to obtain a level of security that is commonly desired – between 8 and 16 selections of each type. This is a burden to the user.

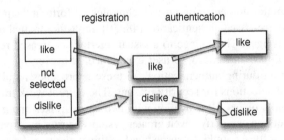

Fig. 5.1 Previous visual preference schemes are based on a registration phase in which a user selects some number of *likes* and *dislikes* – maybe 12 of each – and an authentication phase in which the user identifies the items he likes from his previous selections, displayed in a random order.

At the core of the new solution are two important components. One corresponds to the simple insight that tertiary classification results in greater security than that provided by binary classification; and that with the potential for greater security and fixed expectations, one can reduce the number of items that need to be classified. Here, the three classes are *likes*, *dislikes*, and *no opinions*. Including this third category is known [48] to increase the risk for errors: While it is highly unlikely for a person to make a *like/dislike* classification error, it is much more likely for him to make a *like/no opinion* or *dislike/no opinion* misclassification. To address this practical problem, our solution specifies to the user how many items he needs to classify as *likes* vs. *dislikes* during the authentication session. This is highlighted in figure 5.2, and contrasted in figure 5.1 to the approach used previously.

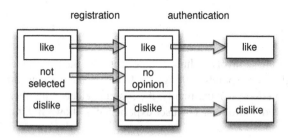

Fig. 5.2 The current visual preference scheme uses a registration phase in which a user selects a relatively small number of *likes* and *dislikes* – maybe 3 of each – and the system infers what selections the user has no strong opinions about. In the authentication phase, the items of these three categories – *likes*, *dislikes*, and *no opinions* – are displayed in a random order, and the user is asked to identify which ones his likes and dislikes. The registration phase becomes faster as a result of the smaller number of selections, compared to previous versions. At the same time, the authentication phase provides higher security due to the use of tertiary, instead of binary, classification.

It is known [48] that most users have an opinion only on a tiny portion of possible selections used in preference-based authentication schemes – and no opinion (or no strong opinion) about the rest. This means that it is reasonable for the system simply to select a collection of items and label them *no opinion*, in order to save the user from having to manually identify all of them during the registration process. Most of the system-selected items would, in fact, belong to the no opinion class. However, some of them may not; worse still, the user may happen to have a strong opinion about one or more of them. This would thwart the authentication process. It is not meaningful to ask the user which ones *he* selected – that would shift the focus back from using preferences to using long-term memory, which would give rise to increased error rates. One possible approach is to allow for some error during the authentication phase – e.g., requiring a threshold of correct answers, but below 100

A second important component of the solution, therefore, is a technique that allows the system to infer what items belong to the *no opinion* class, without explicitly asking the user. In previous incarnations of the system, it has been observed that it is distracting to display too many choices to the user at the same time; to address this, only about 12-15 selections were displayed at any given time. The new system allows the user to refresh this collection if he cannot find any items he likes (or dislikes, depending on the task at hand). From this, it can be inferred what items the user does *not* like; later, the user is shown the same images and asked to identify dislikes. If he refreshes the collection again, he has implicitly stated that he neither likes nor dislikes the current images. These are then placed in the no opinion class.

The experiments we report on next show that we attain an improvement of user experience (in the form of swifter registration and authentication) at the same time as we see a security increase – simply from the subtle changes to the user interface that we have outlined above.

5.4 Solution

The registration phase involves three components: (a) the user selects a small number of images that corresponds to things she likes; (b) then selects a small number of things that she dislikes; (c) and finally, the system selects a number of images that the user is believed not to like. The user experience is shown in figure 5.3.

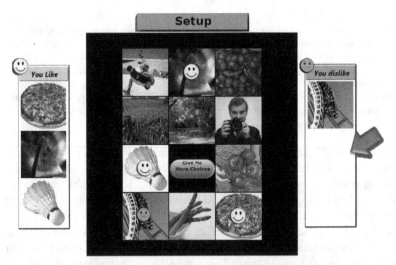

Fig. 5.3 The figure shows a screenshot taken during the registration phase. The user has selected three *likes* (left sidebar) and is about to select three *dislikes* (right sidebar.) Three items among the available selections are marked with a smiley, indicating that the user likes these concepts. One item is marked with a frown, which means that the user dislikes the item. If the user clicks the blinking "Give Me More Choices" button in the center to get more choices, the system notes that the user did not dislike any of the available choices. The system can infer that a user has no opinion about a collection of choices if she indicates in this way that she does not like, or dislike any of the available images.

The *no opinion* images can be inferred from the user's actions as shown in figure 5.4. If a user cannot find any images he likes, he can click on the button on the top of the interface (see figure 5.3); this refreshes the images. It also causes the system to infer that the user does not like any of the images in the previous collection – except for those that he explicitly stated that he liked. Once the user is done with selecting things he likes, he is brought back to the first collection of images that he saw during his selection of *likes*, and is asked to identify those that he dislikes. If the user requests more images at *this* point, the system infers that the user has no strong opinion of any the images in this collection – not counting those for which a preference has been expressed. While this conclusion may be not be perfect – the user may have a slight preference for some, or even a strong preference for one that he did not notice – it raises the quality of the *no opinion* selection without any user effort by making sure that it is very unlikely there are several strong preferences in the no opinion selection. Combined with the use of a threshold comparison during the authentication session, this results in a low risk for errors.

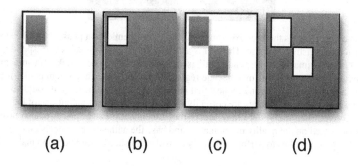

(a)   **(b)**   **(c)**   **(d)**

Fig. 5.4 The figure shows how the system infers no opinion selections. In step (a), the user has selected one item he likes – marked in grey. He then clicks that he needs more images. The unselected images – shown in grey in step (b) – must therefore be either *dislikes* or *no opinion* images. Later on, the user completes the selection of *likes*, and is taken back to the first collection of images to make a selection of *dislikes*. In step (c), he makes one such selection – the grey rectangle in the middle. The grey rectangle in the top corner corresponds to his previously selected like. As the user again requests more images, the system in step (d) infers that the user has no strong opinion of the unselected images – marked in grey. These are therefore added to the *no opinion* class, which is used in the authentication phase.

If a sufficient number of items can be identified as *no opinion* elements using the inference shown in figure 5.4, that concludes the registration process. Otherwise, the system needs to add additional items to the *no opinion* class. This can be done by selecting additional images; especially those for which it is known that the correlation of preferences to the already selected likes and dislikes is particularly low.

The authentication process is straightforward: the user is shown a random ordering of the images in his *like*, *dislike*, and *no opinion* classes, and is asked to select some number of likes; then some number of dislikes – typically the same number as he selects in the registration phase. A typical user experience is shown in figure 5.5.

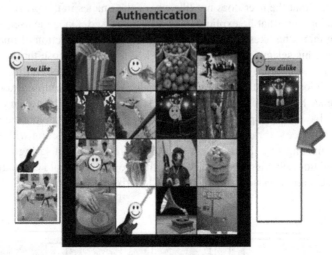

Fig. 5.5 The figure shows the user experience during the authentication phase. Note the strong resemblance to the registration phase. The user is asked to identify what images correspond to things she likes, then what images correspond to things she dislikes. The system makes an authentication decision based on how well this matches the registration selections. The system could, for example, require a perfect alignment and request that the user tries again if he fails. It could also require that a sufficient number of matches are correctly made. For example, if all but one of the likes and dislikes is correct, then the system may accept the authentication attempts. It is also possible to output a score based on the quality of the match, and base the authentication decision on this score and the task the user wishes to perform. We only consider threshold-based decision making herein.

What Does the Adversary Know?

We consider two types of adversaries – what we may call a *simple* adversary and what we call an *informed* adversary. Both know how the protocol works, but neither knows any personal preferences of their victims. The simple adversary does not know anything about the probability distributions of preferences, but the informed adversary knows that each image – if it appears as one of the selections for the authentication phase of an unknown user – belongs to one of the *like*, *dislike* or *no opinion* categories. Similarly, we assume that the informed adversary is aware of the correlations between user selections.

On Bias and Correlation, and How to Avoid Them

If the selection likelihood of some images are is biased, then this gives an informed adversary an advantage in guessing the answer to a given authentication challenge. This is taken into consideration in our design. To begin with, the images were selected to minimize bias. This was done by removing images for which subjects expressed a strong preference either way, and measuring the remaining bias. The remaining bias is measured and taken into consideration in the analysis.

Correlation, as mentioned, can arise from unbalanced probability distributions for images displayed during authentication. The first type of correlation is related to images in very close categories in which a user usually has the same opinion of both images, which we name *related* items. For example, the preferences associated with swimming and water polo are positively correlated. This kind of bias suggests that there is a benefit for attackers to choose *both* these images as either like or dislike. This kind of correlation could be easily resolved if we have a fine-grained categorization hierarchy and do not show images with more than a threshold amount of correlation during the setup phase.

The second type of bias arises from images from multiple selections by a user within one category, even if these images are not normally correlated. For example, a selection including images of drums, a dance floor, and Michael Jackson, and a hot dog, a pizza, and a hamburger suggest a high likelihood that the selection was either made by a food lover who does not enjoy contemporary music, or a music lover who does not like fast food. Of course, it is *possible* that a person likes some of the foods and some of the music items, but dislikes others – but it appears less likely from experimental observations. However, this problem can also be avoided in several ways.

One possible approach is that if a user has chosen too many images within one category (whether as *likes* or *dislikes*), then after she is done with the selections, she is simply asked to select additional images – resulting in a larger number of selections than would otherwise be requested. The second batch of images shown to the user would not include images from the overrepresented categories.

A second approach is to reduce the number of selectable images shown during setup to two images per category. If a user selects both images in one category, then later screens (should the user refresh the available images) would skip this category and offer more images from other categories. Another version of this approach is to replace images from a chosen category with images from unchosen categories in real time. For example, if a user selects a food item images, then the other food item images on the screen would be replaced by other images.

Going forward, we will make the somewhat optimistic assumption that any meaningful amount of correlation is avoided using a collection of approaches like those described above. Theoretically speaking, while this may not be a perfect assumption, we believe that it is a fair approximation for all practical purposes, given the typical approach of online attackers.

5.5 Experiment

To assess the extent to which users manage to authenticate using the proposed system, we performed an experiment.

Phase 1

We used the Amazon Mechanical Turk[2] platform to recruit 400 users with HIT (Human Intelligence Tasks) approval rates of at least 90%. The users were asked to perform an image classification task taking less than one minute, and offered $0.21 in payment for doing so. After completing the registration process, each user was given a unique payment code, which they were asked to enter into the Mechanical Turk response window. Users were not told that they would be given a similar classification test later on to avoid the risk that some users might write down what their selections were.

Identifying Cheaters

To filter out participants who were careless with the assigned task, we asked users to perform the same task during authentication *immediately* after their registeration. The results were only used to identify cheaters, and not to determine how well the subjects would be able to authenticate. Users who made one or more big mistakes or more than two small mistakes were considered cheaters, and not asked to participate in the second phase. Here, a big mistake is a classification of an image *first* as a like, and *later* as a dislike – or the other way around. A small mistake is where the user first classifies an images as a no opinion, and later as a like or dislike – or the other way around. This way, 120 cheaters were detected among the 400 participants, corresponding to a 70% "honesty rate."

Phase 2

Between 6-10 days after registration, Mechanical Turk users were contacted again through the interface and invited to participate in a follow-up study. They were asked to reselect images from the previous registration collections and offered $0.30 for matching a previous selection or $0.10 otherwise.

After the study, the users are told that their answers were not entirely correct (independent of whether they were or not) and asked to re-authenticate.

The study was used to determine the extent to which users successfully authenticate and how much the authentication process was sped up through repetition. It

---

[2] Amazon Mechanical Turk (MTurk) is a crowd-sourcing platform allowing requesters to pay workers to perform small tasks.

also let us verify the extent to which the two sets of authentication attempts helped match user profiles. This is important to know in order to determine the extent to which a leaked profile may give an attacker an advantage in gaining access to other accounts for the same user. Out of the 280 subjects invited, 115 participated.

We Told People They Were Mistaken!

In order to verify whether people improve given a second chance, and how certain they are in their selections, we asked all users retry again after their first attempt to authenticate – no matter how well they did. We told each subject, "You have made at least one mistake. Please try again!"

The experiment showed that 14 out of 115 users did better on their second try. Among these 14, a second try helped only two users' status to change from "non-authenticated" to "authenticated," given the parameter choices detailed later on. Put another way, only two users out of 115 were helped by a second try.

One can also compare the results in the first and second tries to understand how certain users are in their selections. Among the 115, 73 users (63%) did not change their likes during the second try. These users were very certain of their likes. Similarly, 65 users (55%) did not change their dislikes. Finally, 35 users (30%) did not change either their likes or dislikes. All changes were either the result of introducing or removing small mistakes, which led us to conclude that nobody confuses what they truly like with what they truly dislike.

5.6 Analysis

Parameter choices.

In the registration phase, a random permutation was applied to the total of 320 available images. These were grouped into collections of 11, where the user was shown the first such set and asked to choose three likes, followed by three dislikes. If a user pressed the "Give Me More Choices" or the *refresh* button – then the next collection of 11 images was shown. However, the display was "rewinded" back to the first collection (if applicable) when the user was prompted to select dislikes. After the user had selected all her likes and dislikes, the system selected the so-called no opinion images. No opinion images were derived from collections where the user refreshed during the selection of likes and/or dislikes, but which were not selected as either. (An image that was selected at first, but then unselected would not be considered as a no opinion image.)

In our parametrization report, a total of six no opinion images were selected.

In the authentication phase, users were shown a collection of images, including each of the previously selected likes and dislikes (6), and images relegated to no opinion status. The error rates depend on the number of images shown of each type and the threshold of the maximum allowable number of so-called "small mistakes." A small mistake corresponds to a user identification of an item as *like* or *dislike* where the item was classified as *no opinion* by the system; or a user identification of an item as *no opinion* for an item that the system understands to be either a *like* or *dislike* item. In contrast, a *big mistake* is one where a user classifies an item as a *like* when the system has recorded it as a *dislike* – or vice versa.

We report statistics for four parameter choices. Using (L,D,N) to mean the number L of likes, the number D of dislikes, and N to mean the number of no opinion images, we discuss the results from $(L,D,N) = (3,3,6), (3,3,10), (4,4,4), (4,4,8)$, and $(5,5,10)$. using thresholds $T = 2$, $T = 3$, and $T = 4$ for small mistakes.

False negatives.

The error rates depend on the parameters (L,D,N), as well as the threshold T. Figure 5.6 shows the number of small mistakes made by users who made no big mistakes. If $(L,D,N) = (3,3,6)$ and up to two small mistakes were allowed, 96% of users would be successfully authenticated. A higher threshold reduces the false negative rates, allowing a greater number of legitimate users to pass authentication. With the same values for (L,D,N), 100% of users would be authenticated if the system allowed up to three small mistakes. Increasing the threshold, of course, will come at the cost of increased false positives.

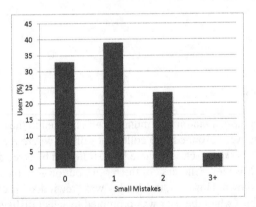

Fig. 5.6 The figure shows the number of small mistakes made in the authentication phase for the parameter choice (L, D, N) = (3, 3, 6). A small mistake is when a no opinion image is chosen as a like or dislike, or vice versa.

We observed that an average of 2.6 likes (86%) are correctly identified during the authentication phase, whereas 2.4 dislikes (80%) are correctly identified. Using a Wilcoxon signed-rank test shows that there is a significant difference between the number of identified likes and dislikes ($W = 465.5$, $Z = -2.48$, $P < 0.01$, $r = 0.23$). It can therefore be concluded that users will be slightly more accurate when identifying their likes than their dislikes. This was not taken into consideration in the scoring of results herein, but more advanced versions could take advantage of this conclusion.

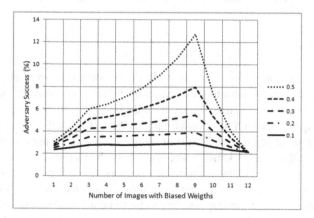

Fig. 5.7 This figure shows how bias in images affects the chances of a successful statistical analysis attack. The parameter selection in the figure is $(L,D,N)_T = (3,3,6)_2$. The x-axis shows the number of images with biased weights for the like and dislike selections, and the y-axis shows an adversary's probable success rate. Each curve shows the adversary's success probability based on a specified bias offset. For example, the curve labeled 0.2 shows the adversary's success probability when the weights of biased images are $(0.43, 0.23, 0.33)$, i.e., there is a difference of 0.2 between the like and dislike probabilities.

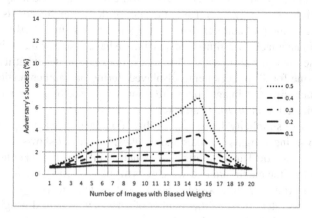

Fig. 5.8 This figure shows the effect of weight bias on an adversary's success probability for $(L,D,N)_T = (5,5,10)_4$. In comparison to the parameter selection $(L,D,N)_T = (3,3,6)_2$ shown in figure 5.7, the success probability here is slightly lower.

Based on the rate of successful identification of likes and dislikes during the authentication phase, one can extrapolate the users' performance for other parameter choices. For example, let's consider $(L,D,N)_T = (5,5,10)_4$. This corresponds to users having to select five likes and dislikes each, with the system adding ten no opinions. When a user authenticates, she is allowed up to $T = 4$ small mistakes, but no big mistakes. The expected success rate of authentication is 99.1%.

False positives.

An adversary can take over an account via the password recovery mechanism if he supplies the right answers to the security questions. This could be achieved by guessing at random and getting lucky. It could be achieved by using statistically aware techniques, in which the attacker applies the statistical distribution of selections by the general population. Finally, it could be achieved by using context aware guesses, where the attacker knows something about the victim.

The success of an attack by a simple attacker depends on the number of no opinion images that are shown in the authentication phase, and the threshold used to determine how accurate the response has to be to be acceptable. For example, using three likes, three dislikes and six no opinion images – what we will refer to as $(L,D,N) = (3,3,6)$ – and an acceptance of up to two small mistakes, an attack by a simple attacker has a 2.1% chance for success; for $(L,D,N)_T = (5,5,10)_4$, 0.5%.

Statistical analysis attacks could take advantage of a known bias in the classification of individual images and a correlation between the categories of images. This can be modeled by assigning each image a skewed selection probability. We will refer to these as *weights*. More specifically, the weight associated with an image in the authentication phase is the probability that this image would be classified in a given manner by an average user. Given some ordering of the images, image i will have weights (w_{iL}, w_{iD}, w_{iN}). Here, the sum of these weights equals 1, and the weights describe the probabilities that the images was classified as *like*, *dislike* and *no opinion*. In an attack by a simple adversary, we have assumed that this vector of weights is the same for all images. Note that it does not matter what it is, as long as it is the same for all images being displayed during one authentication session. However, when different images have different weight vectors, this may translate into an advantage for an *informed* attacker.

For the sake of simplicity, let us assume that all images have a no opinion weight of 0.33, but varying weights for likes and dislikes. Figure 5.7 shows the result of a simulation of a statistical analysis attack, in which an informed attacker first chooses three images with the maximum like-weights as his like selection, then chooses three images with maximum dislike-weights as his dislike selection. The figure shows the probable success rates based on the number of images with biased weights and parameter selection $(L,D,N)_T = (3,3,6)_2$. Compare this to figure 5.8, which shows the effect of weight bias on an adversary's success with a different parameter selection where $(L,D,N)_T = (5,5,10)_4$. It is clear that if an adversary knows much about his victim, then his probability of successful attack increases. , this is not a problem unique to preference questions. In fact, it is a known problem for existing security questions [80] where more than 25% of attackers with personal knowledge of their victims correctly guessed the answer to at least one of the three traditional security questions associated with their victims [75].

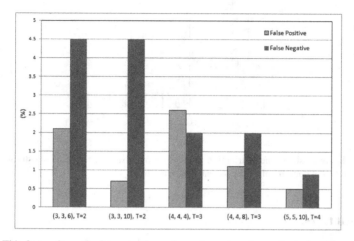

Fig. 5.9 This figure shows the false positive and negative rates of our scheme in different settings of $(L,D,N)_T$. For example, for the parameter choices $(L,D,N)_T = (5,5,10)_4$, the false positive rate is 0.5% and the false negative rate is around 0.9%. The false negatives for other settings are extrapolated from the experiment we described. This assumes consistency with the previously described rates of correct responses for likes and dislikes (86.6% and 80%). The false negatives are calculated by simulating an attack by a simple attacker attack on the proposed system in different setting.

How error rates are affected by the parameter choice.

One can decrease the probability of a successful attack simply by adding some more no opinion images to the authentication phase, or by increasing the number of likes and dislikes – or by reducing the threshold to pass. The benefit of using the number of no opinion images is that this does not affect the time to register – although a drastic increase makes an increase of the threshold necessary to maintain a good balance between false positives and negatives. Using $N = 8$ instead of $N = 6$ for $L = D = 3$ and $T = 2$ causes the probable success rate of an attack by a simple attacker to fall to 1%. Increasing N to 10 brings the probable success rate down to 0.7%. In a setting of $(L,D,N)_3 = (4,4,8)_3$, the probable success rate of the adversary would be 1.1%, when up to three small mistakes are allowed. Figure 5.9 shows the false positive and negative rates for a collection of parameter choices.

An ideal setting in practice is one which keeps both false negative and positives below 1%. Such a setting requires users to identify five likes and dislikes each among ten no opinion images when at most four small mistakes are allowed; in other words, we need a $(L,D,N)_T = (5,5,10)_4$, which has a false negative rate of 0.9% and a false positive of 0.5%.

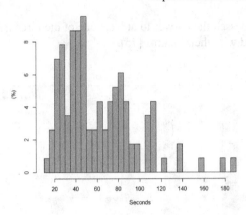

Fig. 5.10 The figure shows the distribution of the time to register. The average registration time is 64 ± 7 seconds, not counting the time to read the instructions.

The time it takes.

Here we report on the time it takes for typical users to read instructions, register, and authenticate. These timings relate to the principal experiment we have described, in which subjects were asked to select three things they like and three things they dislike. The average time for registration – *including* reading instructions – was 83 ± 8 seconds, with a median of 74.4 seconds. Figure 5.10 shows the distribution of the registration time. Registration, not counting the time spent reading instructions, took 64 ± 7 seconds, with a median of 52 seconds. During registration, users spent an average of 11.4 ± 2.2 seconds to choose each like item, and an average of 10.6 ± 1.5 seconds per dislike.

In the authentication phase, subjects took 25 ± 2 seconds, not counting the time spent reading instructions. Users spent an average of 5.1 ± 0.5 seconds per like and 3.6 ± 0.3 seconds for each dislike.

Chapter 6
How to Kill Spoofing

Markus Jakobsson, Hossein Siadati

Abstract

In this chapter, we describe a novel approach to reduce the impact of spoofing by a subtle change in the login process. At the heart of the technique is the understanding that current anti-spoof technologies fail largely as a result of the difficulties to communicate *security* and *risk* to typical users. Accordingly, the approach is *oblivious* to whether the user was tricked by a fraudster or not. This is achieved by modifying the user login process and letting the browser or operating system cause different results of user login requests based on whether the site is trusted or not. Experimental results indicate that the approach, which is dubbed "SpoofKiller," will address approximately 80% of spoofing attempts.

6.1 The Principles of Spoofing – and Spoof Killer

As people interact with each other, they observe cues that indicate the identity of the party they interact with. This is a form of authentication that is implicitly taking place. People also form opinions about the identity and validity of websites as they observe them. Given human inaccuracy, this is a very vulnerable form of authentication, and one that makes *spoofing* possible.

Just as fraudsters may attempt to impersonate a trusted person to an intended victim, they may also *spoof* emails, websites and apps. This is a common technique used by phishers. Phishers use web page spoofing to dupe Internet users into believing that they are visiting trusted websites and giving out their passwords (or other credentials) to these sites.

At the risk of stating the obvious, phishers are only successful if (a) they manage to trick their intended victims, *and* (b) the resulting actions of these victims are beneficial to the fraudsters. Both conditions are necessary.

Typical security measures aim to mitigate the threat of spoofing by addressing the first condition (i.e., keep intended victims from being tricked). This is done by conveying security and risk to users (e.g., using locks and conveying recognizable URLs to represent security) and by issuing warnings and requiring unusual user action to represent risk. This general approach is not very effective as it relies on

M. Jakobsson, *Mobile Authentication*, SpringerBriefs in Computer Science, DOI: 10.1007/978-1-4614-4878-5_6, © The Author(s) 2013

users paying close attention to subtle cues and not acting out of habit. The simple but somewhat ironic beauty of the approach we describe in this chapter is that it turns reflexive user behavior from being a danger, as it is today, to being a distinct *advantage*. When users are habituated to the methods we describe, the very same reactions that currently make these users fail to notice and act on indications of risk are harnessed and made to protect them. The approach taken to achieve this goal relies on undermining the *second* condition for success for phishers, namely that *the resulting actions of victims are beneficial to the fraudsters*.

The approach we describe works by modifying the user login behavior to include an action that generates an interrupt (i.e., pressing the power button). Normally, this interrupt means "terminate" or "turn the screen off and terminate" depending on the phone operating system. By changing that to mean "go ahead" for whitelisted sites – but not for other sites – it is possible to block abuse based on spoofing. As a result, as a user visits a spoofed site – believing she is at a legitimate site – she acts just as she does on legitimate sites. On spoofed sites, this causes the termination of the browser, and therefore also of the offending website. (It is worth mentioning that while malware with root access can spoof the pressing of the power button, a spoofed web page *cannot*; nor can a malicious app without root access.)

The new functionality can easily be achieved by modifying browsers - as demonstrated in a proof-of-concept implementation we describe herein using the open source browser Zirco. In this modified version, which runs on Android devices, the meaning of the power button is changed in the context of whitelisted sites. It could be made simply to mean "go ahead, enter your password now" as in the implementation we describe, or "we have autofilled your user name; now enter your password," to provide a user incentive to make up for the extra button press. However, the meaning of the power button is not changed for other sites. Therefore, if a user presses the power button on a spoof site – not necessarily because she thinks it is a secure site, but simply out of habit – then the browser session will end and the user be brought back to the home screen, because the interrupt handler did not find the URL on the whitelist.

A technique of potential independent value forces users to comply with the new login procedure, all while respecting legacy sites not to have to be aware of our needs and actions. The approach is to let the browser inject javascript in the DOM of the visited site (thereby making it appear that the javascript code was part of the website) where the injected javascript code searches for tags indicative of password fields, and rewrites the website source code to signal the whereabouts of such fields to the browser. If a user attempts to enter text in any such field without first having pressed the power button, the browser will give the user tactile feedback and an alert explaining the need to press the power button on trusted sites. This, in fact, can be the only teaching process by which user behavior is changed.

At first sight, this may seem to mean that a phishing site could modify the HTML to make sure that there would be no tag to trigger the detection of the password field. However, this is a misunderstanding, as the detection of the password field is merely a tool to train the user to press power by recurrent conditioning as the user visits legitimate sites. *Legitimate sites* will not attempt to circumvent the detection of the password field. The abortion of phishing sites does not depend to any extent on the code of the web pages; it is simply a consequence of the user's actions.

Outline.

We begin with a brief overview of related work (section 6.2), after which we describe the psychological principles that our solution is based on (section 6.3). In section 6.4, we describe an implementation of SpoofKiller, followed by an experimental evaluation of it in section 6.5.

6.2 Related Work

The problem of web spoofing was first given attention by Felten, Balfanz, Dean and Wallach [26] years before it was embraced by phishers as a tool of deceit. While credential theft aided by social engineering took place on AOL as early as the midnineties, it was not until 2001 that phishing of the type we are used to today started to appear, first targeting e-gold account holders [32] and then gradually becoming a threat against regular banking. Around 2005, phishing was commonly recognized as a significant problem.

Spoofing is a complex socio-technical problem, and researchers have long studied what typical users pay and *fail* to pay attention to [24, 37, 41, 42, 45, 96, 99]. They have also studied the more general question of what makes people assign trust [49, 56, 76, 90, 94]. Much of this research, sadly, supports what can be understood simply from observing the rising trend of online fraud: *Typical users are not good at making proper online trust decisions.*

To attempt to improve how trust decisions are made, substantial efforts have been made to better convey statements of security to users [16, 23, 31, 38, 64, 100] and more generally, to educate users about the need to pay attention to security indicators [58, 89]. While we are not against such efforts, we think of them as last resorts – approaches to take in the absence of automated protection mechanisms.

In line with this view is a body of work aimed at protecting the user *without* any attempt at messaging [27, 30, 77]. We believe that in order for the system to be reliable, it *should not* depend on the user making proper security decisions. That is the view on which the proposed solution is based.

6.3 Understanding Conditioning

In learning theory, two major classes of learning processes have been identified: *classical conditioning* and *operant conditioning*. In his famous classical conditioning experiment, Pavlov described how dogs learn to associate the ring of a bell (which is referred to as the *conditioned stimulus*) to food (the so-called *unconditioned stimulus*) [40]. While classical conditioning relates to performing actions *in response to* a potential reward or punishment, operant conditioning relates to performing actions intended to *cause or avoid* the reward or punishment. More specifically, operant conditioning identifies how an individual learns that a operant or action may have specific consequences (see, e.g., [29]). As a result of operant conditioning, the individual modifies her behavior to increase the chances of the desired outcome.

Operant conditioning could be used to describe the process by which users learn how to interact with computer systems. For example, a user may learn that a click on an X-icon (operant or action) in a window results in the abortion of the associated application (consequence). Similarly, users of Android devices have learned that pressing the power button terminates an application and locks the phone.

When a user aims to reach a goal the first few times, she performs a collection of actions until the desirable outcome is caused. As the desired consequence occurs (e.g., the user succeeds in locking the phone), the relation to the operant/action (e.g., pressing the power button) is reinforced – we say that she has*learned*.

Similarly, in the context of login, users have learned to enable username and password entries by a click or tap in order to enter her credentials. This is *both* a matter of classical conditioning, where the opportunity to log in is communicated by the display of the login page; and of operant conditioning, where the user knows that by clicking or tapping on the fields, she will be rewarded by the access to her account.

SpoofKiller habituates users to pressing the power button to log in to legitimate sites, using a combination of rewards and punishments. In the context of whitelisted web pages, the *reward* is access to the associated account, while the *punishment* for not pressing the power button consists of tactile feedback and an alert. At the same time, the desirable login action (i.e., the pressing of the power button) is interpreted by the device as a request to terminate the session outside the context of a whitelisted website. Therefore, as soon as users have learned the new login procedure (pressing the power button), they are protected against spoof sites, which will be terminated by this action.

This leaves two important cases to be considered. First , it is evident that good sites that are not whitelisted would potentially suffer the same fate as spoof sites – the termination of the user's session as a result of the user's intention to log in. Apart from requesting to get whitelisted, this problem can be addressed by the operators of such sites by replacing the conditioned stimulus (the login page) with an alert, as shown in Figure 6.1, which makes the user aware of the procedural exception.

A second important question to consider is how fraudsters may react to the threat of having their sessions terminated. One general approach is to display an alert similar to that shown in Figure 6.1, but potentially with even more reassuring messaging. While this may trick some users to proceed, it will at least raise their awareness of the login session being a special case; institutional messaging by whitelisted sites could attempt to minimize this risk by reinforcing that they will *never* ask the user to avoid the power button. Another adversarial strategy is to make the user experience

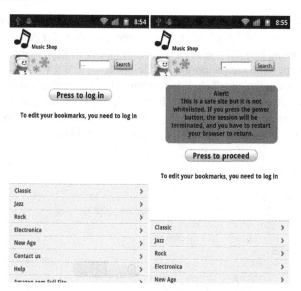

Fig. 6.1 The figure shows how legitimate sites that are not whitelisted can avoid termination. The image on the left shows a regular login screen, which avoids the operant (power press) by removing the conditioned stimulus (the regular login screen). On the right screen, the user is instructed not to press the power button. The actual login screen (not shown above) is not displayed until the user has acknowledged. While many users may *still* press the button right after having made this acknowledgment and being shown the login screen, they will know how to return and try again.

as similar as possible to the real experience (which is typically the path taken by today's spoofers), and hope that the targeted user is not yet conditioned to pressing power, or will somehow fail to do this anyway.

6.4 App Implementation

Typical Android devices are equipped with an array of sensors including the touch screen, means for voice input, GPS, and an accelerometer. The events are delivered from the underlying device drivers to the OS. The OS forwards the events to active applications, or (for events such as location events or incoming calls) broadcasts them as a new *Intent*. Intents are delivered to all subscribed apps – even those that were not active at the time of the event. As a result of the broadcast of an Intent, a subscribing application may be activated. (Apps subscribe to intents by setting up a BroadcastReceiver and its associated intent filters in the manifest of the Android application.) There are two exceptions to this rule. First, the *home button* press is just delivered to the *Launcher*, an application responsible to manage the home screen; second, the *power button* press is not delivered to *any* third party application.

For SpoofKiller to be triggered by the power button, one *either* needs to modify the Android OS to deliver the event to our augmented browser (which would result in complications for us, as it would limit the experiment to users with dev phones), *or* one needs to trigger SpoofKiller using something that is a *consequence* of the power button being pressed – such as the *screen off* event. The latter was done in the proof-of-concept implementation we will describe.

As it is shown in the code below, we registered for the Broadcast event of Screen Off. The onReceive method is called when the Power Press is occurred. As a result, we have an event which is not catchable – or possible to generate – by a web page, and which is used to trigger SpoofKiller to check the whitelist.

```
BroadcastReceiver screenoff =
    new BroadcastReceiver() {

    public static final String Screenoff =
      "android.intent.action.SCREEN_OFF";
    //Indicate what to do
    //when the power is pressed
    @Override
    public void onReceive(
    Context context,Intent intent) {
     //Enable password field
    }};

    //Indicate the type of
    //event interested to receive
    IntentFilter offfilter =
     new IntentFilter (Intent.ACTION_SCREEN_OFF);

    //Application registers
    //to receive screen off event
    registerReceiver(screenoff, offfilter);
}
```

Most Android-based browsers use the WebView class, which is incorporated in the Android WebKit package. This class, given URIs as input, loads and displays the content of associated webpages. In addition to performing standard functionality associated with web browsing, such as running Javascript code and rendering HTML and CSS, WebView allows a web page to call a method of the browser. This functionality, as shown in the code below, allows browser manufacturers to incorporate SpoofKiller in their browsers in a straightforward manner.

```
class JavaScriptInterface {

    @SuppressWarnings("unused")
    public boolean enableSpoofKiller() {
        //set up page to handle Power Press
        //If the page is not in whitelist,
        //this call causes page abortion
    }
}
```

```
mWebView.addJavaScriptInterface(
  new JavaScriptInterface(),
  "spoofkillerhandler");
```

In the code above, the browser provides a JavaScript interface named spoofkiller-handler, which enables JavaScript code in the web page to communicate with SpoofKiller. This lets a web page announce that it wants the support of SpoofKiller on a particular page. (Not all pages on a legitimate website needs the support, but just those that ask for credentials).

We also incorporated other functionality, such as a method to give tactile feedback when a user tries to enter his password without having pressed power first. This has to be triggered by JavaScript in the web page. To support legacy web pages, we have used a technique we call "on the Air Manipulation of Page" (AMP), which enables browsers to modify the contents of the web page by injecting scripting code that determines whether the web page should request SpoofKiller support. This is done simply by injecting a string of JavaScript as a URL to each web page that is loaded. This is done by the browser, a trick that permits access to the document object model (DOM) of the current web page in spite of the fact that the JavaScript code was not *really* served by the domain associated with the web page in question. The code snippet below shows how loading a string of JavaScript as a URL lets us attach an *onclick* event to password elements in a web page.

In the implementation of ZircoSecure – the proof-of-concept browser supporting SpoofKiller – we used the AMP technique to inject JavaScript code in a page loaded in the browser in order to let this injected routine identify fields of importance (using tags) and communicate to the browser when any such field is accessed by the user. This is to accommodate legacy websites while at the same time making sure that whitelisted pages are modified to help the browser identify fields that the user is not allowed to access without first pressing the power button. This, in other words, is what enables the user conditioning described in section 6.3.

The AMP technique makes it possible to deploy SpoofKiller locally without infrastructure changes or modifications of legacy pages. Browser manufacturers – or those writing plugins for browsers – simply need to incorporate *spoofkillerHandler* and the JavaScript injection code into their browsers.

The current implementation of SpoofKiller suffers from screen blackout, since the operating system performs that task as a direct result of detecting an interrupt caused by the power button being pressed. In order to make the SpoofKiller work smoothly and without this undesirable effect, there is a need for a modification of the Android OS. This is a straightforward modification. Using the OTA (over the air update) technology for Android, is is possible to incorporate this with any new release of the Android OS.

6.5 Experimental Evaluation

While one may be convinced that SpoofKiller would work in *theory*, based on known observations on human conditioning, one also need to find heuristic support to back this belief, and to estimate the steepness of the typical learning curve as people start to use SpoofKiller. More specifically, one needs to answer the following questions:

1. Is it practically feasible for users to change a frequently practiced habit, namely the manner in which they log in?
2. How long does it typically take for users to acquire a *new* login behavior, provided initial instructions and appropriate reinforcement?

These two questions relate directly to the practicability and likely user acceptance of the approach. In particular, if the new behavior is commonly embraced and quickly becomes habitual, then this reduces the size of the population that is susceptive to abuse and reduces the risk of corruption for those who have adopted the new behavior. A core question to be answered is then:

3. *What percentage of users would be protected against typical phishing attacks after an initial period of learning?*

To find answers to these questions, we designed and carried out an experiment, which we will describe next.

Experiment Design

We recruited subjects to download and run an experiment app, either from a web page of ours or from Google's Android Marketplace[1]. During setup, we asked subjects to select a username and password – ostensibly so that only *the subject* would have access to his or her environment. Then, subjects were asked to participate in a number of sessions over time, each session having the following two parts:

1. Perform a login, wherein the user name was autofilled, and where the subject had to enter the password; but where he or she had to press the power button before doing so. Unbeknownst to the user, all actions and the time at which they were performed were logged. We will refer to this part as the *authentication phase*.
2. Type three words – chosen at random from a large set of words – as fast as possible. After performing this task, the user would be told how long it took, what his or her average time to date was, and what her ranking was based on speed. This part of the experiment was only there to take the attention away from the first part. (To add to the impression that the timing to typing was what the experiment was about, we named the experiment app *Speed Test*.)

---

[1] Interestingly, many subjects expressed a higher confidence in the Marketplace version, in spite of the absence of any user feedback or any rigid screening.

In the authentication phase, the user was given tactile and textual feedback if she attempted to enter her password without first having pressed the power button. The textual feedback was (in blinking font) *"Notice: For security reasons, you must always press the power button before entering your password in our test."* This constituted the main tool of user conditioning.

Fig. 6.2 The figure shows the Instruction treatment in our experiment, wherein the user is told "Notice: For security reasons, you must always press the power button before entering your password in our test." In the Empty treatment, that instruction is absent, whereas in the Bad treatment the instruction given to the user is instead "Notice: Do not press power. Enter the password you use to log in to [user's email address]."

The experiment had three different *treatments*, all of them providing slightly different versions of what was shown to the user during the authentication phase. We refer to the three treatments as Instruction, Empty, and Bad: The I treatment contained the instruction, *"Notice: For security reasons, you always must press the power button before entering your password in our test,"* as shown in Figure 6.2. The E treatment was identical to the I treatment, except that it did *not* contain this instruction. Finally, the B treatment, had a "bad" instruction, *"Notice: Do not press power. Enter the password you use to log in to [user's email address]."* That last treatment was introduced to determine whether subjects pay attention to instructions after having learned what to do, and if so, whether they were willing to follow an instruction that has the semblance of being abusive.

To be eligible for the participation incentive, subjects had to participate for 21 days out of a month. Many subjects participated in more than one session per day – probably because we emphasized the competitive aspects of the experiment, and many tried hard to improve their speed during the phase where they typed three words. If a subject participated in more than one session per day, all sessions of that day proceeding the first session were chosen as treatment E.

We ran two versions of the experiment, which we may refer to as the *instruction heavy* and the *instruction light* version. In the instruction heavy version, the $\underline{I}$ treatment was the most common, while in the instruction light version, it was only used for a small number of days in the beginning. The aim of using these two experiments was to determine whether the conditioning that we expected to take place was a result of pre-action messaging (i.e., the instruction), post-action reinforcement (whether success or the tactile/textual feedback), or a combination of the two.

More specifically, in the instruction heavy version, the treatment shown to a user was always $\underline{I}$, except on days 9 and 18 in which treatment $\underline{E}$ was used, and on day 21 inn which treatment $\underline{B}$ was used. In contrast, in the instruction light version, $\underline{I}$ was only shown on days 1-5, after which treatment $\underline{E}$ was used until day 21, at which treatment $\underline{B}$ was used.

Subject Recruiting

Before starting to recruit subjects, we attempted to estimate the number of subjects we would need for a desired confidence of 95%. Since the population of the smart phone users is large, we used Cochrans' formula. Based on this, we established that we needed to recruit 385 subjects, given z= 1.96 (i.e., confidence level 95%), e=0.05 (the precision level), p = 0.5 and q = 0.5 (the maximum variability). We assumed maximum variability at first since we did not know to what extent different users behave differently. As we analyzed the results, it became evident that users behave similarly to each other.

The drop-off rates in the unsupervised experiments are different based on the assigned task and reward which are given to the participants. Based on our experience with structurally similar experiments in the past, we assumed an approximate 50% drop-off rate, suggesting the need to recruit close to 800 participants.

Recruitment of such a large number of participants was challenging, given the fact that users had to be over 18 years of age (to comply with guidelines outlined in the Belmont report); have an Android Phone; be willing to install an application; and to participate for 21 days during the course of a month. Moreover, in order to avoid bias, we avoided recruiting anybody who knew what the experiment was about, which excluded some of the otherwise most passionate potential participants.

Instruction Heavy Version.

We recruited subjects by requesting participation from our LinkedIn, Google+, and Facebook contacts. Moreover, we recruited participants among colleagues at PayPal and Google, and from members of HCI research groups. Subjects were incentivized by the chance of winning a raffle for an iPad2[2], with extra raffle tickets given to

---

[2] After plentiful feedback from participants and would-be participants, we changed the raffle prize to the winner's choice of an iPad2 or an Android pad.

people who helped recruit subjects. Out of 198 subjects who registered, 15 entered as a result of a referral. A total of 77 of the 198 registered users completed their participation; 6 of those were due to referrals. All of these users participated in the instruction heavy version of the experiment, which was intended as the only version of the experiment until the disappointing numbers prompted us to recruit another batch of users – at which time we also decided to tweak the experiment to see whether the amount of instructions would matter much.

Instruction Light Version.

In the second round of the experiment, which corresponded to the instruction light version, we recruited workers from Amazon Mechanical Turk to participate[3] and gave them the option of a $5 bonus or the chance to win an iPad/Android pad. Among the 307 who registered, 231 completed the study; more than 90% selected the cash bonus.

Table 6.1 Ages of subjects in the experiment versions

Age Range	Heavy %	Light %	Combined %
18-25	28.1	36.8	33.5
26-32	29.5	34.6	32.7
33-45	28.1	21.9	24.3
46+	14.4	6.6	9.5

Table 6.2 Gender of subjects in experiment versions

Age Range	% Heavy	% Light	% Combined
Female	47.8	24.5	39.0
Male	52.2	75.5	61.0

Demographics.

Tables 6.1 and 6.2 show the breakdown in terms of age and gender among the subjects in our two experiment versions (instruction heavy vs light.) This is very similar to the demographic of the Android phone owners [98, 19]. Table 6.3 shows the experience with entering passwords on handsets of the subjects.

---

[3] It is against the terms of service of Amazon to ask a user to install a piece of software. While we used the payment methods associated with Amazon Mechanical Turk to pay participants, we did not use their services to *recruit* participants, and so, did not break the terms of service. These users had *voluntarily* provided contact information in previous interactions, and were contacted in this manner to ask whether they would like to participate.

Table 6.3 Password use on handsets

Use	% of subjects
Daily	30
Weekly	26
Rarely	33
Never	11

Observation of Actions

The experiment app recorded all the user actions as the user ran our app, including page taps, keyboard presses, and hard-key presses (volume, home, back, menu, and power press) – along with the time at which each such action was performed. It stored the recorded data in a local database on the user handset, then transmitted it to a backend server for analysis. (The data was submitted asynchronously, to make it possible for test takers to take the test when they are offline, and to avoid the data lost in the case of exceptional conditions.)

From the collected data, we could determine the time it took for subjects to press the power button, after starting the authentication phase, and the number and type of actions, if any, that she performed before pressing power.

Findings

Using the data collected in the experiment, we used statistical analysis techniques to answer the questions and validate the hypotheses outlined at the beginning of section 6.5.

Feasibility and Learning Curve.

The cumulative performance, shown in figure 6.3, is a measure of the how quickly subjects adopt to the new behavior. It shows the percentage of subjects performing the correct action – pressing the power button before attempting to log in – as a function of the number of days of participation in the experiment. It shows the performance of subjects in both experiment versions – instruction heavy and instruction light.

The learning curve shown in figure 6.3 is Sigmoid-like for both experiment versions, and the cumulative performance exhibits a dramatic increase during the first few days of participation; we refer to these days as the *acquisition period*, during which user tries different actions (keyboard press, screen touch), and is finally conditioned to performing the correct operant. We can see that the proportion of correct actions is 80% ±5% (with $n = 305, \chi^2 = 0.0461$) for both versions, once the users have acquired the new habit (starting at day 10). We refer to the period starting at

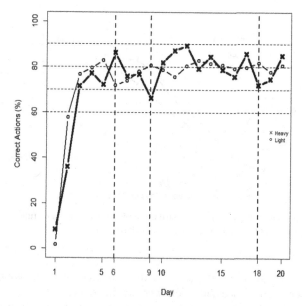

Fig. 6.3 The figure shows the cumulative distribution of the acquisition of the safe habit (pressing power before entering a password) as a function of days of exposure to the new procedure. We see a dip on days 9 and 18 in the heavy version, and one on day 6 for the light version; these all coincide with a sudden $\underline{E}$ treatment after a number of $\underline{I}$ treatments.

that point in time as the *protected period*. The average performance of the users during the protected period is 79.6% ±3%. This is also a measure of the probability with which these users would be protected against a spoofing attack that they would otherwise have fallen for.

A reverse regression model suggests that the cumulative percentage of correct actions is: $88.415 - 76.986/t$, where t denotes the number of days of participation. This suggests a cumulative performance of 87.5% after 84 days with a significance level of 99%.

In the instruction heavy version (n=73), we used the $\underline{E}$ treatment (in which no instruction is provided) on days 9 and 18 in order to determine what portions of subjects have internalized the pressing of the power button by then. Our results show that 52% of the subjects had acquired the secure behavior by day 9, and 72% by day 18. In the light version (n=246), treatment $\underline{E}$ is used from day 6 to day 20. As it can be seen in figure 6.3, the performance is hovering around 80% during this time with a mean of 80% ±1.1%.

The speed with which a user "forgets" an acquired habit is referred to as the *extinction rate*. During the *protected period* (days 10 to 20), the average extinction rate for subjects of the heavy version is 4.70 (n=86), meaning that users make one mistake after 4.70 days on average, and then reacquire the habit again. During the same period, subjects in the light version have an average extinction rate of 5.07 (n=246). See figure 6.4 for a distribution of this aspect of the users' behavior. We argue that

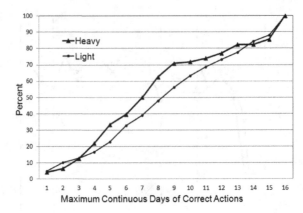

Fig. 6.4 The figure shows the cumulative distribution of the extinction as a function of maximum number of consecutive days of consistently correct behavior.

the instruction light approach is preferable to the instruction heavy approach due to the similar user performance and its cleaner user interface.

We do not believe that the differences in behavior between the instruction heavy and light versions are due to a bias in the choice of subjects – in particular since the instruction light subjects were faster learners, while – coming from Mechanical Turk – are believed to be less likely to care as much as colleagues and friends & family would.

Protection and Prediction.

We want to establish the extent to which practice makes perfect in the context of SpoofKiller – or put another way, how the probability of performing a login action that is "spoof killing" depends on the number of days of exposure.

It is evident that the effects of conditioning are most notable during the first few days of exposure, given the rather rapid learning process (see figure 6.3 above.)

It is also very clear that not all users are equally protected, as can be seen in figure 6.5. Therein we show the results of performing hierarchical clustering on the experimental data based on the subjects' performance during the period we refer to as the "protected period." Three meaningful clusters are detected; we refer to these as the "A students," the "B students," and the "C students," the names indicating the extent to which subjects in these clusters learned the new login procedure. Having made this distinction, it is interesting to see the adoption behavior of the subjects partitioned into these three classes. See figure 6.6. The partition of users into different risk classes, as above, suggests the potential need for additional security measures for users who are identified as being more risk prone – what we refer to as "C students." These are easily detected based on their behavior.

One difficulty facing "C students" is that they do not maintain the desirable behavior when the instruction is removed. This can be seen from figure 6.6, wherein

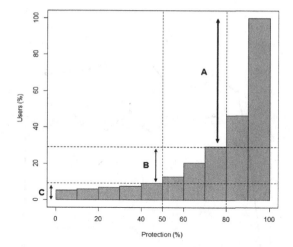

Fig. 6.5 Clustering of users based on their performance during days 10 to 20. We informally refer to the high performers as "A students," the intermediate performers as "B students," and the low performers as "C students."

we see that the performance drops for these subjects after the instruction is removed in the instruction light version on day 6. "C Students" have a very high extinction rate (mean=0.47 days), which means that they have not internalized the desired habit. In comparison, "B students" have an extinction rate of 1.72 days, while "A students," 6.60 days on average. In general, there is a strong correlation (cor=0.7) between a user's performance and the extinction rate.

Fraud Protection

On the last day of the experiment, we used treatment B̲ad, in which users were asked not to press the power button, and to enter their email password instead of the password used in the experiment. (We did not record what password was entered, but only whether the same password was entered as during the previous session; this was to avoid stealing anybody's email password.)

Table 6.4 User behavior in B̲ad treatment (%)

Instruction	Correct	Delayed	Oblivious	Tricked
Heavy	22%	4%	48%	26%
Light	27%	4%	57%	12%
Combined	27%	4%	55%	15%

The B̲ treatment was used to mimic a fraud case. As Table 6.4 shows, roughly 30% of the users pressed the power button – most of them as rapidly as during

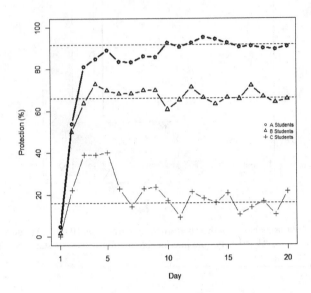

Fig. 6.6 The performance of subjects as a function of time, where the subjects are partitioned into the classes "A students" (70% of all subjects, 92% average performance), "B students" (20% of the subjects, 66% average performance) and "C students" (10% of the subjects, 14% average performance).

"normal" days (the "correct" reaction), and about 4% after a slight delay. The rest of the users did not press the power button. Approximately 55% of the users – independently of whether they pressed the power button or not – entered the same password as previously, oblivious apparently to the request to enter something else, or unwilling to do so. 15% entered something else – supposedly the password to their email account.

Table 6.5 Behavior of classes of users in Bad treatment

Class	Correct	Delayed	Oblivious	Tricked
A Student	29%	3%	55%	11%
B Student	21%	3%	50%	25%
C Student	3%	14%	60%	21%

Table 6.5 shows that A students are better protected in comparison to others in contexts involving deceit.

6.6 User Reactions

After a few days of participation, the added action – to have to press the power button – added less than half a second to the time the login took; see figure 6.7.

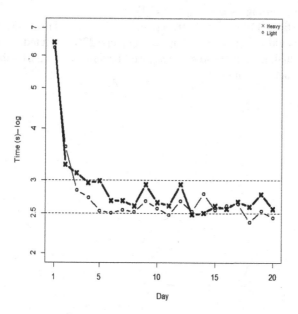

Fig. 6.7 The graph shows the average time for subjects from page rendering to the subject pressing the power button. This is shown as a function of the day of participation. We only show the time for users who perform the correct action. The average reaction time in the protected period (day 10 onwards) for the heavy version is 2.62 seconds, and 2.56 seconds for the light version. In comparison, the user reaction time for similar-style pages, but where the user does not need to press the power button, is 2.5 seconds – the average time for this corresponds to the dotted line. The time associated with pressing the power button is therefore less than half a second.

The reaction time is also a factor of age; younger subjects have shorter reaction time in comparison to older subjects. Table 6.6 shows average speed from page load to power press for different age groups.

Table 6.6 Reaction time for different age groups.

Age Range	Average reaction time (s)
18-25	3.00
26-32	3.50
33-45	3.67
46+	6.25

As subjects completed their participation in their experiment, we asked them what they thought about having to press the power button before logging in with a password. Of the 227 subjects, 127 subjects (56%) selected, "I got used to it quickly," while 24 subjects (11%) selected, "I would have a hard time getting used to that," 76 subjects (33%) expressed neither opinion.

The average performance of users who responded, "I got used to it quickly," (n=112) was not statistically distinguishable from users who responded, "I would have a hard time getting used to that." (n=21)

At the same time, 114 subjects (50%) selected, "If it would provide extra security of any kind, I would be happy to do that," 52 subjects (23%) selected, "I would rather not have to do that, even if it had some security benefit," leaving 61 subjects (27%) who expressed neither opinion.

Chapter 7
Can Biometrics Replace Passwords?

Markus Jakobsson

Abstract

The threat of malware and phishing is engulfing the web. It is expected to be an even greater threat in the mobile context as battery power limitations and the lack of handset screen real estate hinder anti-virus and user messaging methods. In addition, people's continuous handset connectivity makes them more vulnerable to abuse.

This paper argues that biometric methods such as fingerprinting could address a large part of this towering threat - but *only* if properly architected. We describe an architecture that is practically attainable, which would address the problem in a meaningful way, and argue that this is a promising direction – both in terms of security and usability.

7.1 Why We Need Biomterics

Online fraud is assaulting the Internet and its users, and many are concerned that this spiraling problem may suffocate online activity [97]. One aspect of the problem is the increasing ease with which criminals can monetize corrupted accounts, but there are also clear signs of increased sophistication among fraudsters. One such sign is the convergence of methods used by phishers and malware authors. Trojans, for example, increasingly use targeting of victims [2] to improve conversion rates, drawing on lessons learnt by spear phishing artists. Likewise, an increasing portion of malware uses some form of deception to spread and install.

A second worrisome trend is the pace with which both phishers and malware writers are entering the mobile territory and the development of more technically complex attacks. An example of this can be seen in the dual-platform attacks that recently targeted PCs and handsets in coordinated attempts to compromise SMSes used as second factors by banking clients [1]. In the area of Internet fraud, it is becoming hard to see the forest for all the trees.

To have any meaningful chance of turning the trend around, we believe that we cannot afford to address the problem piecemeal, but rather, that we need an overarching solution that is built with an understanding of the entire threat picture. Common to a very large number of fraud instances is the exposure of credentials – whether by users or their devices. This is where we need to focus our attention.

M. Jakobsson, *Mobile Authentication*, SpringerBriefs in Computer Science,
DOI: 10.1007/978-1-4614-4878-5_7, © The Author(s) 2013

We believe that the problem can be mitigated by an increased use of biometrics – a belief shared by many organizations [8]. With processing and storage capabilities, biometric readers can act as secure information wallets. They can be hardened against malware corruption by use of restricted APIs, and be protected against phishing and accidental information disclosure using embedded firmware routines enforcing simple access policies. That said, it is a fallacy to believe that the large-scale deployment of integrated biometric readers would, by itself, eradicate the problem. To make substantial impact, we argue that proper care must be taken to address all special cases; all the way from the physical layer of the biometric reader to the application layer, and *beyond* this, to the manner in which typical users are likely to act and interact.

First of all, the usability issues are immense. If a user relies on a biometric reader *most* of the time, she still needs other forms of authentication such as, standard passwords. However, the user is *almost certain* to forget her passwords between uses if she relies predominantly on biometric authentication. We clearly need a practical backup authentication method that does not deteriorate with infrequent use; one whose security is not so weak as to cause the system security to crumble.

At the same time, it is unreasonable to expect the Internet to be instantly reengineered to accommodate improved security technologies. For years to come, legacy sites will continue to require passwords and be oblivious to the wishes of users to use biometrics. A practical solution must allow such sites to continue to operate, all the while creating an "authentication illusion" in which the early adopter's view is that of an immediate and universal adoption of biometric methods among service providers.

It is also important to recognize physical security concerns. For example, violent criminals may resort to coercion or cutting off fingers if fingerprint readers are deployed. Until we *know* that it is not possible to foil liveness sensors, such concerns must be respected and addressed.

The problem is much greater than first meets the eye, but we argue that it *is* possible to address it – given a proper perspective. This paper proposes a general architecture to address a large array of common types of abuses along with general approaches to address various practical issues. While our proposed approach is not married to any particular biometric authentication technique, we focus on fingerprint readers herein. This is both for reasons of concreteness and in recognition of the recent development of low-cost fingerprint readers with low error rates. We believe that the next few generations of mobile devices and consumer computers will start integrating such readers, and hope that with careful design and engineering, this can become the turning point for Internet security.

7.2 A Brief Overview of Fingerprinting

Fingerprints have been used as a way to identify people for more than 150 years, initially being used along with handwritten signatures on contracts, and later on to identify criminals. With the development of low-cost, high-quality fingerprint readers in the last few years, the technology is starting to enter mainstream authentication, and promises the potential of replacing passwords in many instances.

The science of fingerprints is well-established and goes back to the early 1900s [35]. It is believed that fingerprints start to develop on the fingers and palms of fetuses as early as during the third and fourth month of pregnancy and are complete by the sixth month. While there are general similarities of the fingerprint patterns of family members, and even more notable similarities between the fingerprints of identical twins, all fingerprints are believed to be unique [71]. Fingerprints are expressed both in the epidermal layer –i.e., the outermost layer of the skin– and in the dermal layer, which is inside the epidermal layer.

Fingerprints have three types of patterns – *arches, loops*, and *whorls*. An arch is a pattern where ridges enter on one side of a finger, raise to form an arch, and exit on the other side. A loop pattern corresponds to ridges that enter and exit on the same side of the finger. A whorl is a pattern that swirls around a central point. Fingerprint ridges also have three types of features, referred to as *minutia* . These are *ridge endings, bifurcations*, and *short ridges*.

Fingerprint readers identify *features* – whether patterns or minutia, depending on the algorithm used to process the scanned fingerprint data. There are three main types of hardware approaches used in fingerprint readers– *optical, ultrasonic*, and those based on *capacitance*. An optical reader can be thought of as a camera, taking a photo of the finger. As such, optical fingerprint readers are affected by discolorations of fingers. Ultrasonic and capacitance readers avoid this problem. Ultrasonic readers are based on high frequency sound waves that penetrate the dermal layer and are measured as they reflect off of the epidermal layer. Capacitance readers image the fingerprint by taking advantage of the fact that segments of the ridges act as one plate of a capacitor and the pixels of the sensor array acting as the other.

When a user first registers, a template is produced and stored. The template consists of a collection of features that will later be matched to determine if a person's fingerprint matches the fingerprint of the registered user. Fingerprint matching standards based on so-called *Galton points*–i.e., unique features– vary from country to country. The most common standard is 12 points, as historically used in the US, Australia, France, and the Netherlands. Some countries, like the UK, have higher standards, where a 16 point standard has been in place since 1924. Still, others require fewer points. Sometimes even as few as seven or eight, as is the case in most of Africa.

7.3 Some Concerns to be Addressed

Looking beyond the physical considerations associated with building fingerprint readers with low error rates, there are many issues that need to be addressed to create a practical biometric system – ranging from the mundane to the highly unlikely. Reviewing these in detail, we will understand why it might be neither desirable nor realistic to attempt to *entirely* abandon traditional authentication. We will describe an array of issues of relevance and argue that it is possible to design a practical system that *largely* does away with the need for traditional credentials. Consider the following important issues:

Credential theft. Credentials must be secure against various abuses, including phishing and malware attacks.

Finger theft. While nobody likes the idea of having their password stolen, losing a finger is even less attractive. While there are fingerprint readers that check for the liveness of the tissue, there may always be the nagging question in the minds of would-be users: *can those readers be tricked into accepting a severed finger?* Similarly, it would be better to have a password stolen than be held captive in order to provide fingerprints for authentication. As a result, a mechanism needs to be designed that allows a user to authenticate without fingerprints. This mechanism would be *significantly* less practical than using a fingerprint reader, but would be *more* practical to the rough criminal than kidnapping or finger theft.

Forgotten passwords. The less users rely on passwords, more users will have trouble remembering them when needed, especially under stress. This is a factor we need to be aware of when designing a system that aims largely, but not completely, to do away with passwords.

New device. When a user acquires a new device, her experience should be smooth and intuitive. If a user feels that the task of transferring an established profile from an old device to a new one is too burdensome, this will hamper deployment and cause frustration. On the other hand, it is equally undesirable for a user to register a new device *unintentionally* by simply touching an object with a fingerprint reader that a fraudster has placed in a strategic position. New device registration, in other words, needs to be reasonably simple but not automatic. The authentication used for new device registration could be of the same type as used for the regular authentication (e.g., fingerprinting); using other types of biometrics (e.g., retina scan); or non-biometric methods (e.g., knowledge or possession-based authentication).

Device sharing. The system should preferably support multiple users per device without exposing the credentials of one user to another or leaving one user accidentally logged in after handing the device over to another. This problem exists to some extent already, as some sites may keep users logged in without them being aware of it. However, the problem is made worse by the possibility of authentication that takes place without the user having to be aware of it – although that may be a desirable feature in most situations.

Migration. As technology improves and new readers enter the market, it is important to allow existing users to "roll over" their profiles to take advantage of the better readers – whether this replaces or augments their old profiles.

Legacy systems. For practical deployment reasons, the architecture must be designed with legacy systems in mind. While users authenticate using biometrics, the legacy system will maintain its user name / password structure. Furthermore, when the legacy system demands that a user's password be updated, the user should not be notified of the request.

No fingerprint. Using current consumer technology, 98% of the population have fingerprints that can be reliably read, leaving roughly two in a hundred that do *not* provide reliable fingerprints using today's technology. This number will hopefully shrink over the next few years as technology improves and cost goes down. Nevertheless, those with difficulties or reluctance to use fingerprint readers must be given practical alternatives; another good reason to design with legacy sites in mind.

7.4 A Possible Architecture

To argue for the feasibility of a solution addressing the issues described in the previous section, we outline a possible architecture, followed by sample processes in the next section.

Entities. *Users* interact with *fingerprint readers* embedded in *devices* and facilitate authentication to *service providers* such as apps and websites. We assume that the fingerprint readers have a processor and a small amount of *secure storage* – see figure 7.1 – that is not accessible by malware on the device. Examples of devices include a computer, a handset, a mouse, and a door lock.

Data. A *user profile* contains a user name, one or more templates associated with the user, and a unique decryption key associated with a user-specific secure vault; see figure 7.2. The vault, in turn, contains triplets of domains, user names, and credentials. For legacy sites, the credential may be a password, while it may be a cryptographic key for service providers supporting stronger authentication methods. The vault is an encrypted and authenticated container that can be stored on insecure storage, e.g., he device, and backed up using *cloud storage* or other external storage. See figure 7.3. The vault may also contain other sensitive user information, such as account numbers, social security numbers and health care data.

Data Access. Profiles and vaults can be stored in plaintext on secure storage, which allows them to be read, written, and searched. The secure storage may not be able to store all profiles and vaults that are accessed on a given device at the same time, in which case of these can be stored on insecure storage, such as the device, after having been encrypted and authenticated. For example, one can use AES to encrypt these files one by one, using a key stored on the secured storage. A standard message authentication method such as HMAC [6] can be used for authenticating the

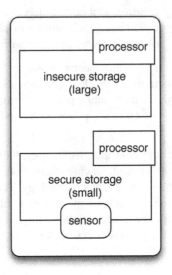

Fig. 7.1 A handset contains two separate components; a large and insecure storage attached to a fast processor (referred to as "the device") and a smaller but secure storage attached to a dedicated processor and a sensor (referred to as the "fingerprint reader"). Users can load apps on the device, but neither users nor software on the device can modify or directly access the contents or components of the fingerprint reader. In particular, the area associated with the secure storage and the fingerprint reader are assumed to be immune to malware infection. Routines may be in firmware. The secure and insecure components are connected by a bus or other interface, and associated with a restricted API.

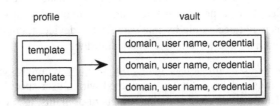

Fig. 7.2 A profile contains one or more templates and is associated with a vault. The vault, in turn, contains triplets specifying a service provider or domain, a user name, and a credential.

encrypted files to avoid modification; again, using a key stored in secure storage. Profiles and vaults can be updated while in secure storage; if this occurs, they are encrypted and MACed before being written back to the insecure storage, which may in turn propagate them to external backup storage.

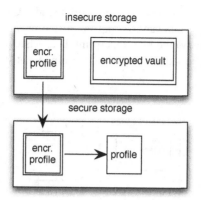

Fig. 7.3 Profiles and vaults are stored in in an encrypted format in insecure storage. They are loaded into secure storage, where they are decrypted.

7.5 Processes

Let us now consider some basic transaction types and how they can be performed:

Authentication. For a user to authenticate to a service provider, she performs a fingerprint scan, which causes her biometric features to be extracted and compared to the templates stored on the fingerprint reader. If a match is found, the associated decryption key is selected by the fingerprint reader and the associated vault loaded and decrypted. The vault is scanned for an entry that matches the selected service provider. If a matching entry is found, the associated domain, user name and credential are extracted. At this point, it is possible to verify the validity of the domain name mapping to harden the system against domain name poisoning [18]. Then, a secure connection is established between the fingerprint reader and the service provider, and the user authenticated. For example, service providers supporting strong user authentication can use mutual SSL. Note that no biometric features or templates are exposed outside the secure perimeter of the fingerprint reader, nor are any user names or credentials.

After the login is successfully completed, the secure session can be handed over from the fingerprint reader to the device in a way that does not allow the device retroactive access to the plaintext data of the transcripts exchanged between the fingerprint reader and the service provider. This can be done by renegotiating SSL keys (see, e.g., [66]) between the fingerprint reader and the website/resource, after which the newly negotiated key can be handed off from the fingerprint reader to the associated device. See figure 7.4. This avoids retroactive credential capture in a setting where the device is infected by malware.

It is worth noting that as long as the fingerprint reader is part of a secure perimeter, it is not possible for malware to "tap in" to the channel from the fingerprint reader and steal (or replay) the raw fingerprint data. Also, phishing is not possible since the processor in the secure area will determine what site gets what credential – if any.

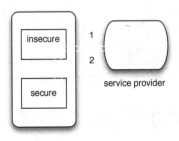

Fig. 7.4 After the user has successfully authenticated to the fingerprint reader, a login is performed to a service provider. Using the device as a proxy, the fingerprint reader negotiates a first SSL connection (labeled 1) with a service provider, over which credentials are exchanged. The proxy then renegotiates SSL (labeled 2), which replaces the old key with a new one. The new key is disclosed to the device, which then seamlessly takes over the connection with the service provider and performs the transaction protected by the authentication. The credentials exchanged during the first SSL connection cannot be accessed by the device, since the key of the renegotiated session is independent of the key of the original session; this provides protection against malware residing on the device.

New device. To register a new device, the user provides an identifier such as a user name or an account number. The new device connects to the cloud storage, provides the user identifier and some form of authentication, and downloads the associated encrypted user template/vault.

The template is decrypted and stored in a secure storage area associated with the fingerprint reader, while the still encrypted vault can be stored in insecure storage on the user's device.

The decryption key can be generated from information the user has/knows or from biometric data – such as features extracted from fingerprinting all ten fingers. It is beneficial to require more arduous fingerprinting for the setup of a new device than having it register when the user thinks she is performing a routine authentication – or worse still, setting off registration simply by touching the device. Moreover, it translates into higher entropy of the decryption keys, which is necessary for cryptographic security of the template.

Backup Authentication. Backup authentication can be implemented in several ways. First, it can be done using alternative biometric approaches, e.g., iris recognition [20] or voice biometrics [65]. Second, if legacy websites retain passwords and password reset mechanisms, this will provide an out-of-band approach for users to access their accounts without using fingerprint readers[1].

We note that it is helpful to implement a form of emergency access that users under duress can use to release the contents of their vaults. This emergency access should be local to a registered device and could work in the same principal way as the new device authentication, except that it should not rely on data that the user might not carry with herself or forget under duress.

Access Policies. Cloud storage can accept backups from multiple devices associated with one and the same account, and synchronize the updates so that all devices get automatically refreshed. Refreshes can also be made in accordance with user-configured restrictions. Such policies may block privileged employer data from being stored on shared personal devices or on any device that was not issued by the employer. In general, it is possible to tie arbitrary policies to the access to and synchronization of software and data, and to tie a license or access rights to a person (and her fingerprint) rather than to a device.

Remote wiping. Remote wiping of a user's template is beneficial, both to "unshare" previously shared devices and to block access to templates and vault contents to criminals with a physical component. It is possible to set policies such as one where a template self-wipes if it is not matched within a particular duration of time. Since user data can be frequently backed up to cloud storage and recovered from this using the new device registration process, it is acceptable to perform a remote wipe when in doubt.

About secure storage. Secure storage is most naturally achieved using dedicated hardware. It can also be achieved using software based attestation (see, e.g., [43, 88]), in which case an external verifier first determines that the device under consideration has no malware, and then provides the decryption key to the encrypted profiles and vaults to the device over a secure connection.

Security Argument. From the above description, it can be seen that the configuration of new devices is relatively easy – but not possible to mistake with regular authentication. Provided suitable backup authentication methods, there should be no reason to fear finger theft, since it is possible for users to bypass the use of biometrics and release the entire contents of their vaults if necessary. At the same time, if data access is limited by policy to employer-issued devices, a criminal would need access to *such* a device to gain access to privileged data – whether he plans to steal a finger or force the release of vault contents of his victim.

The described technology would respect legacy systems, which could maintain a world view of user names and passwords. At the same time though, the passwords could be generated by the fingerprint devices in ways that result in much safer passwords than those produced by typical users while respecting the password formatting rules of sites. Requests to update old passwords can be automatically intercepted and acted on by devices and fingerprint readers. Mutual SSL can easily be

---

[1] It is worth improving the security of these reset mechanisms – independently of the deployment of fingerprint readers – as this is often the weakest link associated with user login [74].

enabled as a stronger alternative to traditional password authentication with secret keys stored in a user's secure vault.

Phishing attempts become largely pointless as credentials are never exposed to sites that do not match the accounts contained in the vault. Moreover, malware is prevented from stealing credentials since PII – whether passwords, keys, templates or biometric features – are never accessible in plaintext outside the fingerprint devices. (However, we note that the threat of malware is *not* entirely neutralized by this move as it is still possible for transaction generators to corrupt sessions that are handed over to the device.)

The resulting automation results both in increased user convenience and improved security.

Chapter 8
Legacy Servers: Teaching Old Dogs New Tricks

Markus Jakobsson, Saman Gerami Moghaddam, Mohsen Sharifi

Abstract

This chapter describes one approach with which legacy systems can be augmented to provide additional functionality. This is a helpful approach to quickly upgrading systems, and to adapt them to new requirements. We describe this in the context of authentication.

8.1 About Legacy Systems and Authentication

New authentication methods typically require significant changes to a codebase residing with the service providers. If the code is well-written and documented, such changes may be relatively simple. Commonly though, the case may be that the engineers who originally wrote the relevant code have long since left the company, and the code they left behind, poorly documented – if at all. In severe cases, the legacy code may have been written in an outdated programming language, or written in a way that does not follow proper guidelines for coding. This makes updates to the codebase practically difficult in many cases. Even if none of these challenges complicate the desired modifications, it is often a great bureaucratic burden to obtain permission to store an extra field in a backend database – simply because every affected part of the organization may need to review the request.

This chapter addresses the question of how these types of complications can be avoided in a modular manner, permitting painless upgrades of authentication mechanisms supported by legacy servers. While this is relevant to any form of authentication, we limit our discussion to the two most common forms of authentication supported by legacy servers: cookies and passwords. Using the approach we describe, new functionality is added in a modular manner along with any associated policies the service provider may wish to implement. The proxy becomes an asynchronous interpreter between the new and the old authentication methods.

Let's first consider HTML cookies, often simply referred to as cookies Cookies have several problems. For one thing, they are sometimes *deleted* – whether by the end user or by her software. Moreover, cookies are commonly *stolen*. Mechanisms such as cache cookies [52] and identification- using user agents [91] are more resistant to these problems. However, new code and fields are required in the database

M. Jakobsson, *Mobile Authentication*, SpringerBriefs in Computer Science,
DOI: 10.1007/978-1-4614-4878-5_8, © The Author(s) 2013

accommodate such measures. See figures 8.1 and 8.2 for an illustration of how this would work.

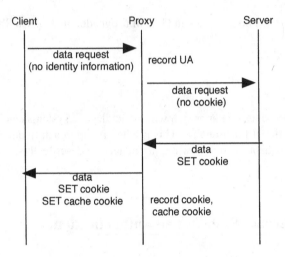

Fig. 8.1 The figure shows the flow when a client device visits the site of a legacy server for the first time. The proxy fails to identify the client and passes on the request. The legacy server responds to the request and sets a cookie. The proxy passes on the response, including the cookie and cache cookie. It stores the information about the cookies along with the user agent of the client device. This triplet constitutes an identifier.

Now, consider a legacy server that relies on passwords, but wishes to use fast-words (described in chapter 4) for user authentication in order to avoid common problems associated with passwords – such as those described in chapter 2. Imagine a proxy sitting between the legacy server and the Internet; therefore, between the legacy server and the client device. This proxy server will *translate* traffic between the legacy server and the client device so that the client device and its user perceives the new authentication mechanism, while the legacy server remains unchanged.

Comparing the two cases, a few differences immediately stand out. First, the translation of cache cookies and the user agent to cookies requires a two-way translation. When the legacy server sets a cookie, the proxy will set an HTML cookie and a cache cookie and then create a new record where the cookies are stored along with the user agent of the client device. Then, when the client device is used to visit a site controlled by the legacy server, the cookies and the user agent are read, the record identified, and the request translated and sent to the legacy server. In contrast, translating fastwords and passwords do not require two-way communication, and therefore, only involves a transcription from a fastword to a password of a format that is acceptable by the legacy server. When a legacy server requests that the user password is updated, this request can either be *propagated* (corresponding to a request for a new fastword), or *suppressed* – in which case the database of the proxy is updated to create the illusion of an update.

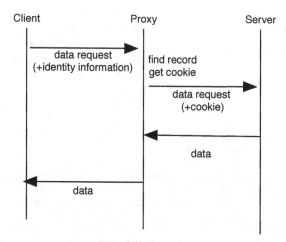

Fig. 8.2 The figure shows the flow when a client device submits a request to a legacy server accompanied by some form of identifying information. The proxy uses this information to identify the associated cookie and passes this along with the request to the legacy server. Note that this is a simplification of the flow. For example, reading a cache cookie may require interaction. Moreover, if not all the identifying information is present, the proxy will set the missing information again by sending a corresponding request to the client device.

An alternative credential translation architecture is described in chapter 7 in the context of biometric authentication, where the proxy is associated with the client device.

8.2 Translating To and From Cookies

The easiest case to consider is a translation between user agents and cookies, since both types of data are automatically communicated with any client request and can be observed by the proxy. Here, the user agent consists of data associated with the browser – such as the browser type and version, the clock skew, and the fonts that are installed. While each of these pieces of information only contributes a small amount of entropy, the *collection* of them is sufficient to identify the device in most cases. Moreover, these types of data rarely change over time. The user of the user agent as a form of identifier is described in a fair amount of detail by Eisen [69].

A cache cookie [52] is an implementation of the typical cookie functionality that uses the client device's browser cache. Unlike user agents, it does not change over time, and like standard HTML cookies, it can only be read by the party that *set* it and deleted by the user clearing her browser cache. One possible implementation of cache cookies is shown in figure 8.3. Cache cookies are not automatically transmitted with GET requests, unless the cache elements are embedded in the referring pages. This adds a potential round of communication in some settings.

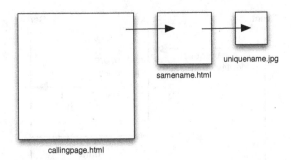

Fig. 8.3 The figure shows the structure of one possible implementation of cache cookies. Cache cookies, like HTML cookies, can be associated with a particular Web page. When a proxy wishes to associate a cache cookie with a Web page, it embeds a request for a second object, samename.html within the calling page. As the cache cookie is set, samename.html is served referring to an object with a unique name for each user; we will refer to that object as uniquename.jpg. The client browser attempts to render samename.html, causing a request for it from the server. The server configures samename.html to the uniquename.jpg, and serves samename.html to the client. For the client browser to render samename.html, it requests uniquename.jpg, which is intentionally not served. As a user returns to callingname.html, the browser again attempts to render the entire page, causing it to load the object samename.html from its cache. As that is rendered, the client browser requests uniquename.jpg, which is not in its cache since it was not served previously. The server still does not serve it, but takes note of the name of the file being requested. This identifies the client device. Note that samename.html can be displayed in a zero-sized iframe, which makes the end user unaware of it being rendered.

By relying on user agent, and cache and HTML cookies to identify the client device, it is much more likely that a machine will be recognized than if only HTML cookies are used.

8.3 Translating Between Fastwords and Passwords

Translating from fastwords to passwords is relatively straightforward. Beginning with the credential establishment, the user may have created the fastword "jog forest squirrel." The proxy would take this credential and perform a mapping of it, where each word is mapped to a representative of its associated word. These representatives may either be synonyms, e.g., resulting in a new triple "run woods squirrel," but could also be something without regular meaning, like the triple "A14 G56 KS2," where each of these three-character combinations correspond to the class to which the associated words belong. A second form of mapping may be removal of blank spaces, resulting in "runwoodssquirrel" or "A14G56KS2." This is done since not all legacy systems allow passwords to contain spaces. Finally, a concatenation of special characters can be made. For example, the character "#" may always be appended at the end, which would result in "runwoodssquirrel#" or "A14G56KS2#," depending on the encoding method. This is done to comply with the password strength rules of the legacy server. Notice that this is not causing a vulnerability, as the fastword already has sufficient entropy, and therefore does not require any special characters. The resulting string is submitted as a password. During login, exactly the same process would be performed. For example, if the user enters the fastword "jogging forest squirrels," these would result in the string "run woods squirrel" – or the non-word version of the same as above. From there on, the rest of the steps are identical to the process for credential establishment As a result, the legacy servers would see the "correct" password and consider the user authenticated.

An interesting aspect to consider is the case in which a legacy server would require a user to update her password – say, after having used it for three months. This causes an outgoing request, which is trapped by the proxy server. Depending on the policies and configurations of the proxy server, this may either propagate a request to the user for her to set a new fastword and then go through the credential establishment process; or to make a modification of the mapping between the user's fastword and password, creating an illusion of the password being updated. For example, instead of concatenating the character "#" at the end, the proxy may insert this character in the second to last position, or concatenate another character, including a random character selected by the proxy and stored in a record associated with the user. The associated new password would then be submitted to the legacy server.

Index

M. Jakobsson, *Mobile Authentication*, SpringerBriefs in Computer Science,
DOI: 10.1007/978-1-4614-4878-5, © The Author(s) 2013

References

1. A. Apvrille. Zeus In The Mobile (Zitmo): Online Bankings Two Factor Authentication Defeated, blog.fortinet.com/zeus-in-the-mobile-zitmo-online-bankings-two-factor-authentication-defeated/.
2. W. Ashford. Hackers turn to online games to target victims, www.computerweekly.com/news/2240105667/hackers-turn-to-online-games-to-target-victims.
3. M. B. B. Ensor and E. Giovannini. How Consumers Remember Passwords.
4. A. Babic, H. Xiong, D. Yao, and L. Iftode. Building robust authentication systems with activity-based personal questions. In *Proceedings of the 2nd ACM workshop on Assurable and usable security configuration*, SafeConfig '09, page 1924, New York, NY, USA, 2009. ACM.
5. G. Bard. Spelling-error tolerant, order-independent pass-phrases via the Damerau-Levenshtein string-edit distance metric. In *Proceedings of the Fifth Australasian Information Security Workshop (Privacy Enhancing Technologies) (AISW 2007)*, 2007.
6. M. Bellare, R. Canetti, and H. Krawczyk. Keying hash functions for message authentication. In *CRYPTO '96: Proceedings of the 16th Annual International Cryptology Conference on Advances in Cryptology*, pages 1–15, London, UK, 1996. Springer-Verlag.
7. S. Berry. One in five use birthday as pin number, Daily Telegraph, 27 Oct 2010.
8. BioAPI Consortium (ANSI/INCITS 358-2002): http://www.bioapi.org.
9. J. Bonneau. Ieee symp. security and pri-vacy. In *The science of guessing: analyzing an anonymized corpus of 70 million passwords*, May 2012.
10. J. Bonneau, M. Just, and G. Matthews. Whats in a name? In R. Sion, editor, *Financial Cryptography and Data Security*, volume 6052 of *Lecture Notes in Computer Science*, pages 98–113. Springer Berlin / Heidelberg, 2010.
11. J. Bonneau, S. Preibusch, and R. Anderson. A birthday present every eleven wallets? the security of customer-chosen banking pins. In *Proceedings of the 16th International Conference on Financial cryptography*, 2012.
12. J. Bonneau, S. Preibusch, and R. Anderson. A birthday present every eleven wallets? the security of customer-chosen banking pins. In *FC '12, The 16th International Conferenceon Financial Cryptography and Data Security*, 2012.
13. W. E. Burr, D. F. Dodson, R. A. Perlner, W. T. Polk, S. Gupta, E. A. Nabbus, C. M. Gutierrez, J. M. Turner, and A. Director. Draft i draft special publication 800-63-1 electronic authentication guideline, 2008.
14. B. Cheswick. Rethinking passwords, www.cheswick.com/ches/talks/rethink-lu.pdf, 2008.
15. G. Chothia, Tom Singh and B. Smyth. Using facebook to reset bank passwords, 2010.
16. N. Chou, R. Ledesma, Y. Teraguchi, and J. C. Mitchell. Client-Side defense against Web-Based identity theft. 2004.
17. A. Cser, J. Penn, P. Stamp, A. Herald, and A. Dill. Identity Management Market Forecast: 2007 To 2014: Provisioning Will Extend Its Dominance Of Market Revenues, www.forrester.com, February 6, 2008.
18. D. Dagon, M. Antonakakis, K. Day, X. Luo, C. P. Lee, and W. Lee. Recursive dns architectures and vulnerability implications. In *NDSS*. The Internet Society, 2009.
19. P. Daniel. Android users demographics, November 19, 2010, http://www.phonearena.com/news/Android-users-demographics_id14786/.
20. J. Daugman. Results from 200 billion iris cross-comparisons. Technical Report UCAM-CL-TR-635, University of Cambridge, Computer Laboratory, June 2005.
21. D. Davis, F. Monrose, and M. K. Reiter. On user choice in graphical password schemes. In *In 13th USENIX Security Symposium*, pages 151–164, 2004.
22. T. Denning, K. Bowers, M. van Dijk, and A. Juels. Exploring implicit memory for painless password recovery. In *Proceedings of the 2011 annual conference on Human factors in computing systems*, CHI '11, page 26152618, New York, NY, USA, 2011. ACM.

23. R. Dhamija and J. D. Tygar. The battle against phishing: Dynamic security skins. In *Proceedings of the 2005 symposium on Usable privacy and security*, SOUPS '05, pages 77–88, New York, NY, USA, 2005. ACM.

24. R. Dhamija, J. D. Tygar, and M. Hearst. Why phishing works. In *Proceedings of the SIGCHI conference on Human Factors in computing systems*, CHI '06, pages 581–590, New York, NY, USA, 2006. ACM.

25. H. Ebbinghaus. Memory: A contribution to experimental psychology, 1885.

26. E. W. Felten, D. Balfanz, D. Dean, and D. S. Wallach. Web spoofing: An internet con game, Technical Report 540-96 (revised Feb. 1997), Department of Computer Science, Princeton University http://www.cs.princeton.edu/sip/pub/spoofing.pdf.

27. I. Fette, N. Sadeh, and A. Tomasic. Learning to detect phishing emails. In *Proceedings of the 16th international conference on World Wide Web*, WWW '07, pages 649–656, New York, NY, USA, 2007. ACM.

28. D. Florencio and C. Herley. A large-scale study of web password habits. In *Proceedings of the 16th international conference on World Wide Web*, WWW '07, pages 657–666, New York, NY, USA, 2007. ACM.

29. E. Fulcher. Cognitive psychology. 2003, http://www.eamonfulcher.com/CogPsych/page5.htm.

30. S. Garera, N. Provos, M. Chew, and A. D. Rubin. A framework for detection and measurement of phishing attacks. In *Proceedings of the 2007 ACM workshop on Recurring malcode*, WORM '07, pages 1–8, New York, NY, USA, 2007. ACM.

31. S. L. Garfinkel and R. C. Miller. Johnny 2: a user test of key continuity management with s/mime and outlook express. In *Proceedings of the 2005 symposium on Usable privacy and security*, SOUPS '05, pages 13–24, New York, NY, USA, 2005. ACM.

32. I. Goldberg. e-gold stomps on phishing?, http://www.financialcryptography.com/mt/archives/000190.html, July, 2004.

33. V. Griffith and M. Jakobsson. Messin' with Texas, Deriving Mother's Maiden Names Using Public Records. In *RSA CryptoBytes*, volume 8(1), pages 18–28, 2007.

34. E. Hayashi, R. Dhamija, N. Christin, and A. Perrig. Use your illusion: secure authentication usable anywhere. In *Proceedings of the 4th symposium on Usable privacy and security*, SOUPS '08, page 3545, New York, NY, USA, 2008. ACM.

35. E. R. Henry. Classification and Uses of Fingerprints (Routledge), 1900.

36. C. Herley, P. C. van Oorschot, and A. S. Patrick. Passwords: If we're so smart, why are we still using them? In *Financial Cryptography*, pages 230–237, 2009.

37. A. Herzberg. Why Johnny can't surf (safely)? Attacks and defenses for web users. *Computers & Security*, pages 63–71, 2009.

38. A. Herzberg and A. Gbara. Security and identification indicators for browsers against spoofing and phishing attacks. Cryptology ePrint Archive, Report 2004/155, 2004.

39. Imperva. Consumer password worst practices, http://www.imperva.com/docs/wp_consumer _password_worst_practices.pdf.

40. G. V. A. Ivan Petrovich Pavlov. *Conditioned reflexes : an investigation of the physiological activity of the cerebral cortex*. Dover Publications, September 2003.

41. C. Jackson, D. R. Simon, D. S. Tan, and A. Barth. An evaluation of extended validation and picture-in-picture phishing attacks. In *Proceedings of the 11th International Conference on Financial cryptography and 1st International conference on Usable Security*, FC'07/USEC'07, pages 281–293, Berlin, Heidelberg, 2007. Springer-Verlag.

42. T. N. Jagatic, N. A. Johnson, M. Jakobsson, and F. Menczer. Social phishing. *Commun. ACM*, 50(10):94–100, 2007.

43. M. Jakobsson and K.-A. Johansson. Practical and Secure Software-Based Attestation. In *Proceedings of LightSec*, 2011.

44. M. Jakobsson and D. Liu. Bootstrapping mobile PINs using passwords. In *W2SP*, 2011.

45. M. Jakobsson and J. Ratkiewicz. Designing ethical phishing experiments: a study of (ROT13) rOnl query features. In *WWW '06: Proceedings of the 15th international conference on World Wide Web*, pages 513–522, New York, NY, USA, 2006. ACM.

46. M. Jakobsson, E. Shi, P. Golle, and R. Chow. Implicit authentication for mobile devices. In *Proceedings of the 4th USENIX conference on Hot topics in security*, HotSec'09, page 99, Berkeley, CA, USA, 2009. USENIX Association.

47. M. Jakobsson, E. Shi, P. Golle, and R. Chow. Implicit authentication for mobile devices. In *HotSec'09: Proceedings of the 4th USENIX conference on Hot topics in security*, pages 9–9, Berkeley, CA, USA, 2009. USENIX Association.

48. M. Jakobsson, E. Stolterman, S. Wetzel, and L. Yang. Love and authentication. In *CHI '08: Proceeding of the twenty-sixth annual SIGCHI conference on Human factors in computing systems*, pages 197–200, New York, NY, USA, 2008. ACM.

49. M. Jakobsson, A. Tsow, A. Shah, E. Blevis, and Y.-K. Lim. What instills trust? a qualitative study of phishing. In *FC'07/USEC'07: Proceedings of the 11th International Conference on Financial cryptography and 1st International conference on Usable Security*, pages 356–361. Springer-Verlag, 2007.

50. M. Jakobsson, L. Yang, and S. Wetzel. Quantifying the security of preference-based authentication. In *DIM '08: Proceedings of the 4th ACM workshop on Digital identity management*, pages 61–70, New York, NY, USA, 2008. ACM.

51. A. Juels. Pets, Weddings, and Identity Theft, December 13, 2006.

52. A. Juels, M. Jakobsson, and T. Jagatic. Cache cookies for browser authentication. In *Security and Privacy, 2006 IEEE Symposium on*, pages 5 pp. –305, May 2006.

53. M. Just. On the design of challenge question systems. *IEEE Security and Privacy*, 2(5):32–39, 2004.

54. M. Just and D. Aspinall. Personal choice and challenge questions: a security and usability assessment. In *Proceedings of the 5th Symposium on Usable Privacy and Security*, SOUPS '09, pages 801–811, New York, NY, USA, 2009. ACM.

55. C.-M. Karat, C. Halverson, D. Horn, and J. Karat. Patterns of entry and correction in large vocabulary continuous speech recognition systems. In *CHI '99: Proceedings of the SIGCHI conference on Human factors in computing systems*, pages 568–575, New York, NY, USA, 1999. ACM.

56. I. Kirlappos and M. A. Sasse. Security education against phishing: A modest proposal for a major re-think. *IEEE Security and Privacy*, 99(PrePrints), 2011.

57. P.-O. Kristensson and S. Zhai. Relaxing stylus typing precision by geometric pattern matching. In *IUI '05: Proceedings of the 10th international conference on Intelligent user interfaces*, pages 151–158, New York, NY, USA, 2005. ACM.

58. P. Kumaraguru, Y. Rhee, S. Sheng, S. Hasan, A. Acquisti, L. F. Cranor, and J. Hong. Getting users to pay attention to anti-phishing education: evaluation of retention and transfer. In *Proceedings of the anti-phishing working groups 2nd annual eCrime researchers summit*, eCrime '07, pages 70–81, New York, NY, USA, 2007. ACM.

59. C. Kuo, S. Romanosky, and L. F. Cranor. Human selection of mnemonic phrase-based passwords. In *Proceedings of the second symposium on Usable privacy and security*, SOUPS '06, pages 67–78, New York, NY, USA, 2006.

60. S. Lee and S. Zhai. The performance of touch screen soft buttons. In *CHI '09: Proceedings of the 27th international conference on Human factors in computing systems*, pages 309–318, New York, NY, USA, 2009. ACM.

61. J. Leyden. Rockyou hack reveals easy-to-crack passwords, http://www.theregister.co.uk/2010/01/21/lamepasswordsexposedbyrockyouhack/, January 21, 2010.

62. I. S. MacKenzie and W. Soukoreff. Text entry for mobile computing: Models and methods, theory and practice. In *Human-Computer Interaction*, volume 17, pages 147–198, 2002.

63. M. Mannan, D. Barrera, C. Brown, D. Lie, and P. C. V. Oorschot. Mercury: Recovering forgotten passwords using personal devices ?

64. J. M. McCune, A. Perrig, and M. K. Reiter. Seeing is believing; using camera phones for human verifiable authentication. *Int. J. Secur. Netw.*, 4:43–56, February 2009.

65. F. Monrose, M. K. Reiter, Q. Li, and S. Wetzel. Cryptographic key generation from voice (extended abstract. In *In Proceeedings of the 2001 IEEE Symposium on Security and Privacy*, pages 12–25, 2001.

66. MozillaWiki. wiki.mozilla.org/security:renegotiation.
67. NIST Special Publication 800-90. Recommendation for Random Number Generation Using Deterministic Random Bit Generators.
68. Y. Niu. *Visual preference authentication. In: Markus Jakobsson, Death of the Internet.* Wiley-IEEE Computer Society, June 2012, pp. 359–369, 2012.
69. E. Oren. *Device Identification and Intelligence.* Wiley-IEEE Computer Society, June 2012, pp. 397–409, 2012.
70. A. PAIVIO, T. B. ROGERS, and P. C. SMYTHE. WHY ARE PICTURES EASIER TO RECALL THAN WORDS? *Psychonomic Science,* 11(4):137–138, 1968.
71. P. Patwari and R. T. Lee. Mechanical control of tissue morphogenesis, Circulation Research 2008, vol. 103 no. 3 pp. 234–243.
72. J. O. Pliam. On the incomparability of entropy and marginal guesswork in brute-force attacks. In *Progress in Cryptology-INDOCRYPT 2000,* 2000.
73. A. Rabkin. Personal knowledge questions for fallback authentication: security questions in the era of facebook. In *Proceedings of the 4th symposium on Usable privacy and security,* SOUPS '08, pages 13–23, New York, NY, USA, 2008. ACM.
74. A. Rabkin. Personal knowledge questions for fallback authentication: security questions in the era of Facebook. In *Proceedings of the 4th Symposium On Usable Privacy and Security,* SOUPS '08, pages 13–23, New York, NY, USA, 2008. ACM.
75. K. Renaud and M. Just. Pictures or questions?: examining user responses to association-based authentication. In *Proceedings of the 24th BCS Interaction Specialist Group Conference,* BCS '10, pages 98–107, Swinton, UK, UK, 2010. British Computer Society.
76. J. Riegelsberger, M. A. Sasse, and J. D. McCarthy. The mechanics of trust: a framework for research and design. *Int. J. Hum.-Comput. Stud.,* 62:381–422, March 2005.
77. B. Ross, C. Jackson, N. Miyake, D. Boneh, and J. C. Mitchell. Stronger password authentication using browser extensions. In *Proceedings of the 14th conference on USENIX Security Symposium - Volume 14,* pages 2–2, Berkeley, CA, USA, 2005. USENIX Association.
78. M. Rothman and B. Wilson. Authentication Death Match: Mobility vs. Passwords (and Why Passwords Will Lose), Webcast, May 17, 2011.
79. S. Schechter, A. J. B. Brush, and S. Egelman. It's no secret: Measuring the security and reliability of authentication via 'secret' questions. In *Proceedings of the 2009 IEEE Symposium on Security and Privacy,* Berkeley, CA, USA, 17 May 2009.
80. S. Schechter, A. J. B. Brush, and S. Egelman. It's no secret. measuring the security and reliability of authentication via secret questions. In *In Proceedings of IEEE Symposium on Security and Privacy,* pages 375–390, 2009.
81. S. Schechter, C. Herley, and M. Mitzenmacher. Popularity is everything: A new approach to protecting passwords from statistical-guessing attacks. In *Proceedings of HotSec 2010,* 2010.
82. S. Schechter and R. W. Reeder. 1 + 1 = you: measuring the comprehensibility of metaphors for configuring backup authentication. In *Proceedings of the 5th Symposium on Usable Privacy and Security,* SOUPS '09, page 9:19:31, New York, NY, USA, 2009. ACM.
83. S. Schechter, S Egelman and R. Reeder. It's not what you know, but who you know: A social approach to last-resort authentication. In *Proceedings of the SIGCHI conference on Human Factors in Computing Systems,* CHI '09, Boston, MA, USA, 2009.
84. S. E. Schechter, A. J. B. Brush, and S. Egelman. It's no secret. measuring the security and reliability of authentication via "secret" questions. In *IEEE Symposium on Security and Privacy,* pages 375–390. IEEE Computer Society, 2009.
85. B. Schneier. Myspace passwords aren't so dumb.
86. B. Schneier. The Curse of the Secret Question, February 11, 2005.
87. C. E. Shannon. Prediction and entropy of printed English. *Bell Systems Technical Journal,* 30:50–64, 1951.
88. E. Shi, A. Perrig, and L. V. Doorn. Bind: A fine-grained attestation service for secure distributed systems. In *SP '05: Proceedings of the 2005 IEEE Symposium on Security and Privacy,* pages 154–168, Washington, DC, USA, 2005. IEEE Computer Society.

89. S. Srikwan and M. Jakobsson. Using cartoons to teach Internet security. *Cryptologia*, 32(2):137–154, 2008.

90. F. Stajano and P. Wilson. Understanding scam victims: seven principles for systems security. *Commun. ACM*, 54:70–75, Mar. 2011.

91. the41. the41. http://www.the41.com/.

92. Voiceport. Password Reset, last retrieved in June 2008.

93. K. Wang, C. Thrasher, E. Viegas, X. Li, and B.-j. P. Hsu. An overview of microsoft web n-gram corpus and applications. In *Proceedings of the NAACL HLT 2010 Demonstration Session*, HLT '10, pages 45–48, Morristown, NJ, USA, 2010. Association for Computational Linguistics.

94. R. Wash. Folk models of home computer security. In *Proceedings of the Sixth Symposium on Usable Privacy and Security*, SOUPS '10, pages 11:1–11:16, New York, NY, USA, 2010. ACM.

95. D. Weinshall. Cognitive authentication schemes safe against spyware. In *Security and Privacy, 2006 IEEE Symposium on*, pages 6 pp. –300, May 2006.

96. T. Whalen and K. M. Inkpen. Gathering evidence: use of visual security cues in web browsers. In *Proceedings of Graphics Interface 2005*, GI '05, pages 137–144, School of Computer Science, University of Waterloo, Waterloo, Ontario, Canada, 2005. Canadian Human-Computer Communications Society.

97. P. Windley. Michael Barrett on Web 2.0: This stuff scares the hell out of me, www.zdnet.com/blog/btl/michael-barrett-on-web-20-this-stuff-scares-the-hell-out-of-me/6889.

98. L. Woolston. Mobclix index: Android marketplace, November 17, 2010, http://blog.mobclix.com/2010/11/17/mobclix-index-android-marketplace/.

99. M. Wu, R. C. Miller, and S. L. Garfinkel. Do security toolbars actually prevent phishing attacks? In *Proceedings of the SIGCHI conference on Human Factors in computing systems*, CHI '06, pages 601–610, New York, NY, USA, 2006. ACM.

100. M. Wu, R. C. Miller, and G. Little. Web wallet: preventing phishing attacks by revealing user intentions. In *Proceedings of the second symposium on Usable privacy and security*, SOUPS '06, pages 102–113, New York, NY, USA, 2006. ACM.

101. J. Yan, A. Blackwell, R. Anderson, and A. Grant. Password memorability and security: empirical results. *IEEE Security & Privacy Magazine*, 2(5):25–31, Sept. 2004.

102. M. Zviran and W. J. Haga. User authentication by cognitive passwords: an empirical assessment. In *JCIT: Proceedings of the fifth Jerusalem conference on Information technology*, pages 137–144, Los Alamitos, CA, USA, 1990. IEEE Computer Society Press.